The Color *of* Water

The Color
of Water

A BLACK MAN'S TRIBUTE
TO HIS WHITE MOTHER

James McBride

BLOOMSBURY

First published in Great Britain 1998

Bloomsbury Publishing Plc
38 Soho Square
London, W1V 5DF

First published in the USA 1996 by Riverhead Books

Copyright © 1996 by James McBride

The moral right of the author has been asserted

A copy of the CIP entry for this book is available from the British Library

ISBN 0 7475 3831 X

10 9 8 7 6 5 4 3 2 1

Printed in Great Britain by Clays Ltd, St Ives plc

I wrote this book for my mother,
and her mother, and mothers everywhere.

In memory of Hudis Shilsky,
Rev. Andrew D. McBride,
and Hunter L. Jordan, Sr.

Contents

As a boy, I never knew where my mother was from—where she was born, who her parents were. When I asked she'd say, "God made me." When I asked if she was white, she'd say, "I'm light-skinned," and change the subject. She raised twelve black children and sent us all to college and in most cases graduate school. Her children became doctors, professors, chemists, teachers—yet none of us even knew her maiden name until we were grown. It took me fourteen years to unearth her remarkable story—the daughter of an Orthodox Jewish rabbi, she married a black man in 1942—and she revealed it more as a favor to me than out of any desire to revisit her past. Here is her life as she told it to me, and betwixt and between the pages of her life you will find mine as well.

The Color *of* Water

1.

Dead

I'm dead.

You want to talk about my family and here I been dead to them for fifty years. Leave me alone. Don't bother me. They want no parts of me and me I don't want no parts of them. Hurry up and get this interview over with. I want to watch Dallas. See, my family, if you had a been part of them, you wouldn't have time for this foolishness, your roots, so to speak. You'd be better off watching the Three Stooges than to interview them, like to go interview my father, forget it. He'd have a heart attack if he saw you. He's dead now anyway, or if not he's 150 years old.

I was born an Orthodox Jew on April 1, 1921, April Fool's Day, in Poland. I don't remember the name of the town where I was born, but I do remember my Jewish name: Ruchel Dwajra Zylska. My parents got rid of that name when we came to America and changed it to Rachel Deborah Shilsky, and I got rid of that name when I was nineteen and never used it again after I left Virginia for good in 1941. Rachel Shilsky is dead as far as I'm concerned. She had to die in order for me, the rest of me, to live.

My family mourned me when I married your father. They said kaddish and sat shiva. That's how Orthodox Jews mourn their dead. They say prayers, turn their mirrors down, sit on boxes for seven days, and cover their heads. It's a real workout, which is maybe why I'm not a Jew now. There were too many rules to follow, too many forbiddens and "you can'ts" and "you mustn'ts," but does anybody say they love you? Not in my family we didn't. We didn't talk that way. We said things like, "There's a box in there for the nails," or my father would say, "Be quiet while I sleep."

My father's name was Fishel Shilsky and he was an Orthodox rabbi. He escaped from the Russian army and snuck over the Polish border and married my mother in an arranged marriage. He used to say he was under fire when he ran off from the army, and his ability to slick himself out of anything that wasn't good for him stayed with him for as long as I knew him. Tateh, we called him. That means father in Yiddish. He was a fox, especially when it came to money. He was short, dark, hairy, and gruff. He wore a white shirt, black pants, and a tallis on his shirtsleeve, and that was like his uniform. He'd wear those black pants till they glazed and shined and were ripe enough to stand in the corner by themselves, but God help you if those pants were coming your way in a hurry, because he was nobody to fool with, my father. He was hard as a rock.

My mother was named Hudis and she was the exact opposite of him, gentle and meek. She was born in 1896 in the town of Dobryzn, Poland, but if you checked there today, nobody would remember her family because any Jews who didn't leave before Hitler got through with Poland were wiped out in the Holocaust. She was pretty about the face. Dark hair, high cheekbones, but she had polio. It paralyzed her left side and left her in overall poor health. Her left hand was useless. It was bent at the wrist and held close to her chest. She was nearly blind in her left eye and walked with a severe limp, dragging her left foot behind her. She was a quiet woman, my sweet Mameh. That's what we called her, Mameh. She's one person in this world I didn't do right by. . . .

2.

The Bicycle

When I was fourteen, my mother took up two new hobbies: riding a bicycle and playing piano. The piano I didn't mind, but the bicycle drove me crazy. It was a huge old clunker, blue with white trim, with big fat tires, huge fenders, and a battery-powered horn built into the middle of the frame with a button you pushed to make it blow. The contraption would be a collector's item now, probably worth about five thousand dollars, but back then it was something my stepfather found on the street in Brooklyn and hauled home a few months before he died.

I don't know whether it was his decision to pull out or not, but I think not. He was seventy-two when he died, trim, strong, easygoing, seemingly infallible, and though he was my stepfather, I always thought of him as Daddy. He was a quiet, soft-spoken man who wore old-timey clothes, fedoras, button-down wool coats, suspenders, and dressed neatly at all times, regardless of how dirty his work made him. He did everything slowly and carefully, but beneath his tractorlike slowness and outward gentleness was a crossbreed of quiet Indian and country black man, surefooted, hard, bold, and quick. He took no guff and gave none. He married my mother, a white Jewish woman, when she had eight mixed-race black children, me being the youngest at less than a year old. They added four more children to make it an even twelve and he cared for all of us as if we were his own. "I got enough for a baseball team," he joked. One day he was there, the next—a stroke, and he was gone.

I virtually dropped out of high school after he died, failing every class. I spent the year going to movies on Forty-second Street in Times Square with my friends. "James is going through his revolution," my siblings snickered. Still, my sisters were concerned, my older brothers angry. I ignored them. Me and my hanging-out boys were into the movies. Superfly, Shaft, and reefer, which we smoked in as much quantity as possible. I snatched purses. I shoplifted. I even robbed a petty drug dealer once. And then in the afternoons, coming home after a day of cutting school, smoking reefer, waving razors, and riding the subway, I would see my mother pedaling her blue bicycle.

She would ride in slow motion across our street, Murdock Avenue in the St. Albans section of Queens, the only white person in sight, as cars swerved around her and black motorists gawked at the strange, middle-aged white lady riding her ancient bicycle. It was her way of grieving, though I didn't know it then. Hunter Jordan, my stepfather, was dead. Andrew McBride, my biological father, had died while she was pregnant with me fourteen years earlier. It was clear that Mommy was no longer interested in getting married again, despite the efforts of a couple of local preachers who were all Cadillacs and smiles and knew that she, and thus we, were broke. At fifty-one she was still slender and pretty, with curly black hair, dark eyes, a large nose, a sparkling smile, and a bowlegged walk you could see a mile off. We used to call that "Mommy's madwalk," and if she was doing it in your direction, all hell was gonna break loose. I'd seen her go up to some pretty tough dudes and shake her fist in their faces when she was angry—but that was before Daddy died. Now she seemed intent on playing the piano, dodging bill collectors, forcing us into college through sheer willpower, and riding her bicycle all over Queens. She refused to learn how to drive. Daddy's old car sat out front for weeks, parked at the curb. Silent. Clean. Polished. Every day she rode her bike right past it, ignoring it.

The image of her riding that bicycle typified her whole existence to me. Her oddness, her complete nonawareness of what the world thought of her, a nonchalance in the face of what I perceived to be imminent danger from blacks and whites who disliked her for being a white person in a black world. She saw none of it. She rode so slowly that if you looked at her from a distance it seemed as if she weren't moving, the image frozen, painted against the spring sky, a middle-aged white woman on an antique bicycle with black kids zipping past her on Sting-Ray bikes and skateboards, popping wheelies and throwing baseballs that whizzed past her head, tossing firecrackers that burst all around her. She ignored it all. She wore a flower-print dress and black loafers, her head swiveling back and forth as she rode shakily past the triangle curve where I played stickball with my friends, up Lewiston Avenue, down the hill on Mayville Street where a lovely kid named Roger got killed in a car accident, back up the hill on Murdock, over the driveway curb, and to the front of our house. She would stop, teetering shakily, catching herself just before the bike collapsed onto the sidewalk. "Whew!" she'd say, while my siblings, camped on the stoop of our house to keep an eye on her, shook their heads. My sister Dotty would say, "I sure wish you wouldn't ride that bike, Ma," and I silently agreed, because I didn't want my friends seeing my white mother out there riding a bicycle. She was already white, that was bad enough, but to go out and ride an old bike that went out of style a hundred years ago? And a grown-up no less? I couldn't handle it.

As a boy, I always thought my mother was strange. She never cared to socialize with our neighbors. Her past was a mystery she refused to discuss. She drank tea out of a glass. She could speak Yiddish. She had an absolute distrust of authority and an insistence on complete privacy which seemed to make her, and my family, even odder. My family was huge, twelve kids, unlike any other family I'd ever seen, so many of us that at times Mommy would call us by saying, "Hey James—Judy-Henry-Hunter-Kath—whatever your name is, come here a minute." It wasn't that she forgot who we were, but there were so many of us, she had no time for silly details like names. She was the commander in chief of my house, because my stepfather did not live with us. He lived in Brooklyn until near the end of his life, staying away from the thronging masses to come home on weekends, bearing food and tricycles and the resolve to fix whatever physical thing we had broken during the week. The nuts and bolts of raising us was left to Mommy, who acted as chief surgeon for bruises ("Put iodine on it"), war secretary ("If somebody hits you, take your fist and *crack* 'em"), religious consultant ("Put God first"), chief psychologist ("Don't think about it"), and financial adviser ("What's money if your mind is empty?"). Matters involving race and identity she ignored.

As a kid, I remember wishing I were in the TV show *Father Knows Best*, where the father comes home from work every day wearing a suit and tie and there are only enough kids to fit on his lap, instead of in my house, where we walked around with huge holes in our pants, cheap Bo-Bo sneakers that cost $1.99 at John's Bargains store, with parents who were busy and distracted, my stepfather appearing only on weekends in sleeveless T-shirt, tools in hand, and Mommy bearing diapers, pins, washcloths, Q-tips, and a child in each arm with another pulling at her dress. She barely had time to wipe the behind of one child before another began screaming at the top of her lungs. Back in the Red Hook Housing Projects in Brooklyn, where we lived before moving to the relative bliss of St. Albans, Queens, Mommy put us to bed each night like slabs of meat, laying us out three and four to a bed, one with his head to the headboard, the next with his feet to the headboard, and so on. "Head up, toes down," she called it as she kissed us good night and laid us out in the proper position. The moment she left the room we'd fight over who got to sleep next to the wall. "I got the inside!" I'd shout, and Richard, the brother above me and thus my superior, would shake his head and say, "No, no, no. *David* sleeps on the inside. *I* have the middle. *You*, knucklehead, have the outside," so all night I'd inhale David's breath and eat Richie's toes, and when I couldn't stand the combination of toes and breath any longer I'd turn over and land on the cold cement floor with a clunk.

It was kill or be killed in my house, and Mommy understood that, in fact created the system. You were left to your own devices or so you thought until you were at your very wits' end, at which time she would step in and rescue you. I was terrified when it came my turn to go to school. Although P.S. 118 was only eight blocks away, I wasn't allowed to walk there with my siblings because kindergarten students were required to ride the bus. On the ill-fated morning, Mommy chased me all around the kitchen trying to dress me as my siblings laughed at my terror. "The bus isn't bad," one quipped, "except for the snakes." Another added, "Sometimes the bus never brings you home." Guffaws all around.

"Be quiet," Mommy said, inspecting my first-day-of-school attire. My clothes were clean, but not new. The pants had been Billy's, the shirt was David's, the coat had been passed down from Dennis to Billy to David to Richie to me. It was a gray coat with a fur collar that had literally been chewed up by somebody. Mommy dusted it off with a whisk broom, set out eight or nine bowls, poured oatmeal in each one, left instructions for the eldest to feed the rest, then ran a comb through my hair. The sensation was like a tractor pulling my curls off. "C'mon," she said, "I'll walk you to the bus stop." Surprise reward. Me and Mommy alone. It was the first time I remember ever being alone with my mother.

It became the high point of my day, a memory so sweet it is burned into my mind like a tattoo, Mommy walking me to the bus stop and every afternoon picking me up, standing on the corner of New Mexico and 114th Road, clad in a brown coat, her black hair tied in a colorful scarf, watching with the rest of the parents as the yellow school bus swung around the corner and came to a stop with a hiss of air brakes.

Gradually, as the weeks passed and the terror of going to school subsided, I began to notice something about my mother, that she looked nothing like the other kids' mothers. In fact, she looked more like my kindergarten teacher, Mrs. Alexander, who was white. Peering out the window as the bus rounded the corner and the front doors flew open, I noticed that Mommy stood apart from the other mothers, rarely speaking to them. She stood behind them, waiting calmly, hands in her coat pockets, watching intently through the bus windows to see where I was, then smiling and waving as I yelled my greeting to her through the window. She'd quickly grasp my hand as I stepped off the bus, ignoring the stares of the black women as she whisked me away.

One afternoon as we walked home from the bus stop, I asked Mommy why she didn't look like the other mothers.

"Because I'm not them," she said.

"Who are you?" I asked.

"I'm your mother."

"Then why don't you look like Rodney's mother, or Pete's mother? How come you don't look like me?"

She sighed and shrugged. She'd obviously been down this road many times. "I do look like you. I'm your mother. You ask too many questions. Educate your mind. School is important. Forget Rodney and Pete. Forget their mothers. You remember school. Forget everything else. Who cares about Rodney and Pete! When they go one way, you go the other way. Understand? When they go one way, you go the other way. You hear me?"

"Yes."

"I know what I'm talking about. Don't follow none of them around. You stick to your brothers and sisters, that's it. Don't tell nobody your business neither!" End of discussion.

A couple of weeks later the bus dropped me off and Mommy was not there. I panicked. Somewhere in the back of my mind was the memory of her warning me, "You're going to have to learn to walk home by yourself," but that memory blinked like a distant fog light in a stormy sea and it drowned in my panic. I was lost. My house was two blocks away, but it might as well have been ten miles because I had no idea where it was. I stood on the corner and bit back my tears. The other parents regarded me sympathetically and asked me my address, but I was afraid to tell them. In my mind was Mommy's warning, drilled into all twelve of us children from the time we could walk: "Never, ever, ever tell your business to nobody," and I shook my head no, I don't know my address. They departed one by one, until a sole figure remained, a black father, who stood in front of me with his son, saying, "Don't worry, your mother is coming soon." I ignored him. He was blocking my view, the tears clouding my vision as I tried to peer behind him, looking down the block to see if that familiar brown coat and white face would appear in the distance. It didn't. In fact there wasn't anyone coming at all, except a bunch of kids and they certainly didn't look like Mommy. They were a motley crew of girls and boys, ragged, with wild hairdos and unkempt jackets, hooting and making noise, and only when they were almost upon me did I recognize the faces of my elder siblings and my little sister Kathy who trailed behind them. I ran into their arms and collapsed in tears as they gathered around me, laughing.

3.

Kosher

My parents' marriage was put together by a rov, a rabbi of a high order who goes to each of the parents and sees about the dowry and arranges the marriage contract properly according to Jewish law, which meant love had nothing to do with it. See, my mother's family had all the class and money. Tateh, I don't know where his family was from. Mameh was his meal ticket to America, and once he got here, he was done with her. He came here under the sponsorship of my mother's eldest sister, Laurie, and her husband, Paul Schiffman. You couldn't just walk into America. You had to have a sponsor, someone who would say, "I'll vouch for this person." He came first and after a few months sent for his family—me, Mameh, and my older brother, Sam. I was two years old and Sam was four when we arrived, so I don't remember anything about our long, perilous journey to America other than what I've seen in the movies. I *have a legal paper in the shoebox under my bed that says I arrived here on August 23, 1923, on a steamer called the Austergeist. I kept that paper on my person wherever I went for over twenty years. That was my protection. I didn't want them to throw me out. Who? Anybody . . . the government, my father, anybody. I thought they could throw you out of America like they throw you out of a baseball game. My father would say, "I'm a citizen and you're not. I can send you back to Europe anytime I want." He used to threaten us with that, to send us back to Europe, especially my mother, because she was the last of her family to get here and she had spent a good deal of her life running from Russian soldiers in Poland. She used to talk about the Czar or the Kaiser and how the Russian soldiers would come into the village and line up the Jews and shoot them in cold blood. "I had to run for my life," she used to say. "I held you and your brother in my arms as I ran." She was terrified of Europe and happy to be in America.*

When we first got off the boat we lived with my grandparents Zaydeh and Bubeh on 115th and St. Nicholas in Manhattan. Although I was a tiny child, I remember Zaydeh well. He had a long beard and was jolly and always seemed to be drinking hot tea out of a glass. All the men in my family had long beards. Zaydeh kept a picture of himself and my grandmother on his bureau. It was taken while they were in Europe. They were standing side by side, Zaydeh wearing a black suit, with a hat and beard, and Bubeh wearing a wig, or shaytl, as was the religious custom. Bubeh was bald underneath that wig, I believe. That's why women were supposed to keep their heads covered. They were bald.

I enjoyed my grandparents. They were warm and I loved them the way any grandchild loves a grandparent. They kept a clean, comfortable apartment, furnished with heavy dark mahogany pieces. Their dining room table was covered with a sparkling white lace tablecloth at all times. They were strictly Orthodox and ate kosher every day. You don't know anything about kosher. You think it's a halvah candy bar. You need to read up on it because I ain't no expert. They got folks who write whole books about it, go find them and ask them! Or read the Bible! Shoot! Who am I? I ain't nobody! I can't be telling the world this! I don't know! The way we did it, you had dif-

ferent table settings for every meal, different tablecloths, different dishes, forks, spoons, knives, everything. And you couldn't mix your meals. Like you had your dairy meals and your meat meals. So you eat all dairy one meal and all meat the next. No mixing it up. No pork, either—no pork chops with potato salad, no bacon and eggs, forget all that. You sit your butt down and eat what you were supposed to, and do what you were supposed to. We used a special-type tablecloth for dairy meals because you could clean it with a simple dishrag as opposed to washing it. Then every Friday evening at sundown you had to light your candles and pray and the Sabbath began. That lasted till sundown Saturday. No light switches could be turned on or off, no tearing of paper, no riding in cars or going to the movies, not even a simple thing like lighting a stove. You had to sit tight and read by candlelight. Or just sit tight. For me that was the hardest thing, sitting tight. Even as a girl, I was a runner. I liked to get out of the house and go. Run. The only thing I was allowed to do on the Sabbath was read romance magazines. I did that for years.

I remember when Zaydeh died in the apartment. I don't know how he died, he just died. In those days people didn't linger and fool around like people do now, with tubes hanging out their mouths and making doctors rich and all this. They just died. Dead. Bye. Well, he was dead, honey. They laid him out on his bed and brought us children into his bedroom to look at him. They had to lift me and my brother Sam off the floor to see him. His beard lay flat on his chest and his hands were folded. He had a little black tie on. He seemed asleep. I remember saying to myself that he couldn't possibly be dead, because it seemed not too long before that he'd been alive and joking and being silly and now here he was dead as a rock. They buried him before sundown that day and we sat shiva for him. All the mirrors in the house were covered. The adults covered their heads. Everyone sat on boxes. My grandmother wore black for a long time afterwards. But you know, I felt they were burying him too quick. I wanted to ask someone, "Suppose Zaydeh isn't dead? Suppose he's joking and wakes up to find out he's buried?" But a child in my family didn't ask questions. You did what you were told. You obeyed, period.

I always remembered that, and I think that's why I'm claustrophobic today, because I didn't know what death was. You know my family didn't talk of death. You weren't allowed to say the word. The old-time Jews, they'd spit on the floor when they said the word "death" in Yiddish. I don't know if it was superstition or what, but if my father said "death" you can bet two seconds later spit would be flying out his mouth. Why? Why not! He could throw up on the floor in his house and no one was allowed to say a word to him. Why he'd spit I do not know, but when my grandfather passed away I kept asking myself, "Suppose Zaydeh isn't dead, then what? And he's surrounded by all those dead people too, and he's still alive?" Lord . . . anything that's too closed in makes me feel like I can't breathe and I'm going to die. That's why I tell y'all to make sure I'm dead when I die. Kick me and pinch me and make sure I'm gone, because the thought of being buried alive, lying there all smushed up and smothered and surrounded by dead people and I'm still alive, Lord, that scares me to death.

4.

Black Power

When I was a boy, I used to wonder where my mother came from, how she got on this earth. When I asked her where she was from, she would say, "God made me," and change the subject. When I asked her if she was white, she'd say, "No. I'm light-skinned," and change the subject again. Answering questions about her personal history did not jibe with Mommy's view of parenting twelve curious, wild, brown-skinned children. She issued orders and her rule was law. Since she refused to divulge details about herself or her past, and because my stepfather was largely unavailable to deal with questions about himself or Ma, what I learned of Mommy's past I learned from my siblings. We traded information on Mommy the way people trade baseball cards at trade shows, offering bits and pieces fraught with gossip, non-sense, wisdom, and sometimes just plain foolishness. "What does it matter to you?" my older brother Richie scoffed when I asked him if we had any grandparents. "You're adopted anyway."

My siblings and I spent hours playing tricks and teasing one another. It was our way of dealing with realities over which we had no control. I told Richie I didn't believe him.

"I don't care if you believe me or not," he sniffed. "Mommy's not your real mother. Your real mother's in jail."

"You're lying!"

"You'll see when Mommy takes you back to your real mother next week. Why do you think she's been so nice to you all week?"

Suddenly it occurred to me that Mommy *had* been nice to me all week. But wasn't she nice to me all the time? I couldn't remember, partly because within my confused eight-year-old reasoning was a growing fear that maybe Richie was right. Mommy, after all, did not really look like me. In fact, she didn't look like Richie, or David—or any of her children for that matter. We were all clearly black, of various shades of brown, some light brown, some medium brown, some very light-skinned, and all of us had curly hair. Mommy was, by her own definition, "light-skinned," a statement which I had initially accepted as fact but at some point later decided was not true. My best friend Billy Smith's mother was as light as Mommy was and had red hair to boot, but there was no question in my mind that Billy's mother was black and my mother was not. There was something inside me, an ache I had, like a constant itch that got bigger and bigger as I grew, that told me. It was in my blood, you might say, and however the notion got there, it bothered me greatly. Yet Mommy refused to acknowledge her whiteness. Why she did so was not clear, but even my teachers seemed to know she was white and I wasn't. On open school nights, the question most often asked by my schoolteachers was: "Is James adopted?" which always prompted an outraged response from Mommy.

I told Richie: "If I'm adopted, you're adopted too."

"Nope," Richie replied. "Just you, and you're going back to your real mother in jail."

"I'll run away first."

"You can't do that. Mommy will get in trouble if you do that. You don't want to see Ma get in trouble, do you? It's not her fault that you're adopted, is it?"

He had me then. Panic set in. "But I don't want to go to my real mother. I want to stay here with Ma . . ."

"You gotta go. I'm sorry, man."

This went on until I was in tears. I remember pacing about nervously all day while Richie, knowing he had ruined my life, cackled himself to sleep. That night I lay wide awake in bed waiting for Mommy to get home from work at two A.M., whereupon she laid the ruse out as I sat at the kitchen table in my tattered Fruit of the Loom underwear. "You're not adopted," she laughed.

"So you're my real mother?"

"Of course I am." Big kiss.

"Then who's my grandparents?"

"Your grandpa Nash died and so did your grandma Etta."

"Who were they?"

"They were your father's parents."

"Where were they from?"

"From down south. You remember them?"

I had a faint recollection of my grandmother Etta, an ancient

black woman with a beautiful face who seemed very confused, walking around with a blue dress and a fishing pole, the bait, tackle, and
line dragging down around her ankles. She didn't seem real to me.

"Did you know them, Ma?"

"I knew them very, very well."

"Did they love you?"

"Why do you ask so many questions?"

"I just want to know. Did they love you? Because your own parents
didn't love you, did they?"

"My own parents loved me."

"Then where are they?"

A short silence. "My mother died many, many years ago," she said.
"My father, he was a fox. No more questions tonight. You want some
coffee cake?" Enough said. If getting Mommy's undivided attention
for more than five minutes was a great feat in a family of twelve kids,
then getting a midnight snack in my house was a greater thrill. I cut
the questions and ate the cake, though it never stopped me from wondering, partly because of my own growing sense of self, and partly because of fear for her safety, because even as a child I had a clear sense
that black and white folks did not get along, which put her, and us, in
a pretty tight space.

In 1966, when I was nine, black power had permeated every element of my neighborhood in St. Albans, Queens. Malcolm X had
been killed the year before and had grown larger in death than in life.
Afros were in style. The Black Panthers were a force. Public buildings,
statues, monuments, even trees, met the evening in their original bland
colors and reemerged the next morning painted in the sparkling "liberation colors" of red, black, and green. Congas played at night on the
streets while teenyboppers gathered to talk of revolution. My siblings
marched around the house reciting poetry from the Last Poets, a sort

of rap group who recited in-your-face poetry with conga and fascinating vocal lines serving as a musical backdrop, with songs titled
"The Revolution Will Not Be Televised" and "On the Subway." Every
Saturday morning my friends and I would pedal our bicycles to the
corner of Dunkirk Street and Ilion Avenue to watch the local drag
racers near the Sun Dew soft drink factory, trying to see who could
drive the fastest over a dip in the road that sent even the slowest-
moving car airborne. My stepfather hit that dip at fifteen miles an
hour in his '64 Pontiac and I bounced high in my seat. These guys hit
it at ninety and their cars flew like birds, barreling through the air and
landing fifteen feet away, often skidding out of control, sometimes
smacking against the wall of the Sun Dew factory before wobbling
away in a pile of bent metal, grilles, and fenders. Their cars had names
like "Smokin' Joe" and "Miko" and "Dream Machine" scrawled on
the hoods, but our favorite was a gleaming black, souped-up GTO
with the words "Black Power" written in smooth white script across
the hood and top. It was the fastest and its driver was, of course, the
coolest. He drove like a madman, and after leaving some poor
Corvette in the dust, he'd power his mighty car in a circle, wheel it
around, and do a victory lap for us, driving by at low speed, one muscled arm angling out the window, his car rumbling powerfully, while
we whistled and cheered, raising our fists and yelling, "Black power!"
He'd laugh and burn rubber for us, tires screeching, roaring away in a
burst of gleaming metal and hot exhaust, his taillights flashing as he
disappeared into the back alleyways before the cops had a chance to
bust him. We thought he was God.

But there was a part of me that feared black power very deeply for
the obvious reason. I thought black power would be the end of my
mother. I had swallowed the white man's fear of the Negro, as we were
called back then, whole. It began with a sober white newsman on our

black-and-white television set introducing a news clip showing a Black Panther rally, led by Bobby Seale or Huey Newton or one of those young black militant leaders, screaming to hundreds and hundreds of angry African-American students, "Black power! Black power! Black power!" while the crowd roared. It frightened the shit out of me. I thought to myself, *These people will kill Mommy.* Mommy, on the other hand, seemed unconcerned. Her motto was, "If it doesn't involve your going to school or church, I could care less about it and my answer is no whatever it is."

She insisted on absolute privacy, excellent school grades, and trusted no outsiders of either race. We were instructed never to reveal details of our home life to any figures of authority: teachers, social workers, cops, storekeepers, or even friends. If anyone asked us about our home life, we were taught to respond with, "I don't know," and for years I did just that. Mommy's house was an entire world that she created. She appointed the eldest child at home to be "king" or "queen" to run the house in her absence and we took it from there, creating court jesters, slaves, musicians, poets, pets, and clowns. Playing in the street was discouraged and often forbidden and if you did manage to slip out, "Get your butt in this house before dark," she would warn, a rule she enforced to the bone. I often played that rule out to its very edge, stealing into the house at dusk, just as the last glimmer of sunlight was peeking over the western horizon, closing the door softly, hoping Mommy had gone to work, only to turn around and find her standing before me, hands on hips, whipping belt in hand, eyes flicking angrily back and forth to the window, then to me, lips pursed, trying to decide whether it was light or dark outside. "It's still light," I'd suggest, my voice wavering, as my siblings gathered behind her to watch the impending slaughter.

"That looks like light to you?" she'd snap, motioning to the window.

"Looks pretty dark," my siblings would chirp from behind her. "It's definitely dark, Ma!" they'd shout, stifling their giggles. If I was lucky a baby would wail in another room and she'd be off, hanging the belt on the doorknob as she went. "Don't do it again," she'd warn over her shoulder, and I was a free man.

But even if she had any interest in black power, she had no time to talk about it. She worked the swing shift at Chase Manhattan Bank as a typist, leaving home at three P.M. and returning around two A.M., so she had little time for games, and even less time for identity crises. She and my father brought a curious blend of Jewish-European and African-American distrust and paranoia into our house. On his end, my father, Andrew McBride, a Baptist minister, had his doubts about the world accepting his mixed family. He always made sure his kids never got into trouble, was concerned about money, and trusted the providence of the Holy Father to do the rest. After he died and Mommy remarried, my stepfather, Hunter Jordan, seemed to pick up where my father left off, insistent on education and church. On her end, Mommy had no model for raising us other than the experience of her own Orthodox Jewish family, which despite the seeming flaws—an unbending nature, a stridency, a focus on money, a deep distrust of all outsiders, not to mention her father's tyranny—represented the best and worst of the immigrant mentality: hard work, no nonsense, quest for excellence, distrust of authority figures, and a deep belief in God and education. My parents were nonmaterialistic. They believed that money without knowledge was worthless, that education tempered with religion was the way to climb out of poverty in America, and over the years they were proven right.

Yet conflict was a part of our lives, written into our very faces, hands, and arms, and to see how contradiction lived and survived in its essence, we had to look no farther than our own mother. Mommy's contradictions crashed and slammed against one another like bumper cars at Coney Island. White folks, she felt, were implicitly evil toward blacks, yet she forced us to go to white schools to get the best education. Blacks could be trusted more, but anything involving blacks was probably slightly substandard. She disliked people with money yet was in constant need of it. She couldn't stand racists of either color and had great distaste for bourgeois blacks who sought to emulate rich whites by putting on airs and "doing silly things like covering their couches with plastic and holding teacups with their pinkies out." "What fools!" she'd hiss. She wouldn't be bothered with parents who bragged about their children's accomplishments, yet she insisted we strive for the highest professional goals. She was against welfare and never applied for it despite our need, but championed those who availed themselves of it. She hated restaurants and would not enter one even if the meals served were free. She actually preferred to be among the poor, the working-class poor of the Red Hook Housing Projects in Brooklyn, the cement mixers, bakers, doughnut makers, grandmothers, and soul-food church partisans who were her lifelong friends. It was with them that she and my father started the New Brown Memorial Baptist Church, a small storefront church which still stands in Red Hook today. Mommy loves that church and to this day still loves Red Hook, one of the most dangerous and neglected housing projects in New York City. On any given day she'll get up in the morning, take the New Jersey Transit train from her home in Ewing, New Jersey, to Manhattan, then take the subway to Brooklyn, and wander around the projects like the Pope, the only white person in sight, waving to friends, stepping past the drug addicts, smiling at the young mothers pushing their children in baby carriages, slipping into the poorly lit hallway of 80 Dwight Street while the young dudes in hooded sweatshirts stare balefully at the strange, bowlegged old white lady in Nikes and red sweats who slowly hobbles up the three flights of dark, urine-smelling stairs on arthritic knees to visit her best friend, Mrs. Ingram in apartment 3G.

As a boy, I often found Mommy's ease among black people surprising. Most white folks I knew seemed to have a great fear of blacks. Even as a young child, I was aware of that. I'd read it in the paper, between the lines of my favorite sport columnists in the *New York Post* and the old *Long Island Press*, in their refusal to call Cassius Clay Muhammad Ali, in their portrayal of Floyd Patterson as a "good Negro Catholic," and in their burning criticism of black athletes like Bob Gibson of the St. Louis Cardinals, whom I idolized. In fact I didn't even have to open the paper to see it. I could see it in the faces of the white people who stared at me and Mommy and my siblings when we rode the subway, sometimes laughing at us, pointing, muttering things like, "Look at her with those little niggers." I remember when a white man shoved her angrily as she led a group of us onto an escalator, but Mommy simply ignored him. I remember two black women pointing at us, saying, "Look at that white bitch," and a white man screaming at Mommy somewhere in Manhattan, calling her a "nigger lover." Mommy ignored them all, unless the insults threatened her children, at which time she would turn and fight back like an alley cat, hissing, angry, and fearless. She had a casual way of ignoring affronts, slipping past insults to her whiteness like a seasoned boxer slips punches. When Malcolm X, the supposed demon of the white man, was killed, I asked her who he was and she said, "He was a man ahead of his time." She actually liked Malcolm X. She put him in nearly the same category as her other civil rights heroes, Paul Robeson, Jackie Robinson, Eleanor Roosevelt, A. Philip Randolph, Martin Luther King, Jr., and the Kennedys—any Kennedy. When Malcolm X talked about "the white devil" Mommy simply felt those references didn't apply to her. She viewed the civil rights achievements of black Americans with pride, as if they were her own. And she herself occasionally talked about "the white man" in the third person, as if she had nothing to do with him, and in fact she didn't, since most of her friends and social circle were black women from church. "What's the matter with these white folks?" she'd muse after reading some craziness in the *New York Daily News*. "They're fighting over this man's money now that he's dead. None of them wanted him when he was alive, and now look at them. Forget it, honey"—this is Mommy talking to the newspaper—"your husband's dead, okay? He's dead— poop! You had your chance. Is money gonna bring him back? No!" Then she'd turn to us and deliver the invariable lecture: "You don't need money. What's money if your mind is empty! Educate your mind! Is this world crazy or am I the crazy one? It's probably me."

Indeed it probably was—at least, I thought so. I knew of no other white woman who would board the subway in Manhattan at one o'clock every morning and fall asleep till she got to her stop in Queens forty-five minutes later. Often I could not sleep until I heard her key hit the door. Her lack of fear for her safety—particularly among blacks, where she often stuck out like a sore thumb and seemed an easy target for muggers—had me stumped. As a grown man, I understand now, understand how her Christian principles and trust in God kept her going through all her life's battles, but as a boy, my faith was not that strong. Mommy once took me to Harlem to visit my stepsister, Jacqueline, whom we called Jack and who was my father's daughter by a previous marriage and more like an aunt than a sister. The two of them sat in Jack's parlor and talked into the night while Jack cooked big plates of soul food, macaroni and cheese, sweet potato pies, and biscuits for us. "Take this home to the kids, Ruth," Jack told Ma. We put the food in shopping bags and took it on the subway without incident, but when we got off the bus in St. Albans near our house, two black men came up behind us and one of them grabbed Mommy's purse. The shopping bag full of macaroni and cheese and sweet potato pies burst open and food flew everywhere as Mommy held on to her purse, spinning around in a crazy circle with the mugger, neither saying a word as they both desperately wrestled for the purse, whirling from the sidewalk into the dark empty street like two ballerinas locked in a death dance. I stood frozen in shock, watching. Finally the mugger got the purse and ran off as his buddy laughed at him, and Mommy fell to the ground.

She got up, calmly took my hand, and began to walk home without a word.

"You okay?" she asked me after a few moments.

I nodded. I was so frightened I couldn't speak. All the food that Jack had cooked for us lay on the ground behind us, ruined. "Why didn't you scream?" I asked, when I finally got my tongue back.

"It's just a purse," she said. "Don't worry about it. Let's just get home."

The incident confirmed my fears that Mommy was always in danger. Every summer we joined the poor inner-city kids the Fresh Air Fund organization sent to host families or to summer camps for free. The luckier ones among my siblings got to stay with host families, but I had to go to camps where they housed ten of us in a cabin for two weeks at a time. Sometimes they seemed closer to prison or job corps than camp. Kids fought all the time. The food was horrible. I was constantly fighting. Kids called me Cochise because of my light skin and curly hair. Despite all that, I loved it. The first time I went, Mommy took me to the roundup point, a community center in Far Rockaway, once the home of middle-class whites and Jews like playwright Neil Simon, but long since turned black, and it seemed that the only white person for miles was my own mother. The camp organizers set up a table inside where they removed our shoes and shirts and inspected our toes for athlete's foot, checked us for measles and chicken pox, then sent us outside to board a yellow school bus for the long journey to upstate New York. As I sat on the bus peering out the window at Mommy, the only white face in a sea of black faces, a black man walked up with his son. He had a mustache and a goatee and wore black leather pants, a black leather jacket, a ton of jewelry, and a black beret. He seemed outstandingly cool. His kid was very handsome, well dressed, and quite refined. He placed his kid's bags in the back of the bus and when the kid went to step on the bus, instead of hugging the child, the father offered his hand, and father and son did a magnificent, convoluted black-power soul handshake called the "dap," the kind of handshake that lasts five minutes, fingers looping, thumbs up, thumbs down, index fingers collapsing, wrists snapping, bracelets tingling. It seemed incredibly hip. The whole bus watched. Finally the kid staggered breathlessly onto the bus and sat behind me, tapping at the window and waving at his father, who was now standing next to Mommy, waving at his kid.

"Where'd you learn that handshake?" someone asked the kid.

"My father taught me," he said proudly. "He's a Black Panther."

The bus roared to life as I panicked. A Black Panther? Next to Mommy? It was my worst nightmare come true. I had no idea who the Panthers truly were. I had swallowed the media image of them completely.

The bus clanked into gear as I got up to open my window. I wanted to warn Mommy. Suppose the Black Panther wanted to kill her? The window was stuck. I tried to move to another window. A counselor grabbed me and sat me down. I said, "I have to tell my mother something."

"Write her a letter," he said.

I jumped into the seat of the Black Panther's son behind me—his window was open. The counselor placed me back in my seat.

"Mommy, Mommy!" I yelled at the closed window. Mommy was waving. The bus pulled away.

I shouted, "Watch out for him!" but we were too far away and my window was shut. She couldn't hear me.

I saw the Black Panther waving at his son. Mommy waved at me. Neither seemed to notice the other.

When they were out of sight, I turned to the Black Panther's son sitting behind me and punched him square in the face with my fist. The kid held his jaw and stared at me in shock as his face melted into a knot of disbelief and tears.

5.

The Old Testament

My father was a traveling preacher. He was just like any traveling preacher except he was a rabbi. He wasn't any different from the rest of those scoundrels you see on TV today except he preached in synagogues and he wasn't so smooth-talkin'. He was hard as a rock and it didn't take long before the Jewish congregations figured him out and sent him on his way, so we traveled a lot when I was a young girl. In those days any Orthodox Jew who said he was a rabbi could preach and go around singing like a cantor and such. That's all some of those Jews could do in those days, travel around and preach and sing. There weren't jobs out there like you know them today. Living. That was your job. Surviving. Reading the Old Testament and hoping it brought you something to eat, that's what you did.

See, Orthodox Jews work with contracts. Or at least my family did. A contract to marry. A contract to preach. A contract for whatever. Money was part of their lives because they had nothing else, like a real home. At least we didn't. Tateh would sign a contract with a synagogue and after a year the synagogue wouldn't renew it, so we'd pack up and move to the next town. We lived in so many places I can't remember them. Glens Falls, New York; Belleville, New Jersey; Port Jervis, New York; Spring-field, Massachusetts; someplace called Dover. I remember Belleville because someone was always giving us hand-me-down clothes there. That's how the members from the congregations would pay us, with food and a place to stay and their cast-off clothes. I remember Springfield, Massachusetts, because my sister Gladys was born there. We called her Dee-Dee. She was four years younger than me. Dee-Dee came into this world around 1924. Whether she is still in this world today I do not know. She would be the last of my mother's children still alive other than me.

We carted everything we had from town to town by bus—clothes, books, hats, and these huge quilts my mother had brought from Europe. They were full of goose feathers. You call them piezyna, in Jewish. They were warm as a house. My sister and I slept under them wherever we lived. We attracted a lot of attention when we traveled because we were poor and Jewish and my mother was handicapped. I was real conscious of that. Being Jewish and having a handicapped mother. I was ashamed of my mother, but see, love didn't come natural to me until I became a Christian.

For a while we lived above a Jewish store in Glens Falls, in upstate New York, and the kind Jewish people who ran it baked us pies and gave us apples. We went sled-ding and did things as a family and my parents seemed to get along. It wasn't bad up there really, but as usual Tateh's contract didn't get renewed and we had to leave. Luckily he got an offer to run a synagogue in Suffolk, Virginia. He told Mameh, "We're moving south." Mameh didn't want to go. She said, "Maybe we can get some-thing up here," because her sisters and her mother were in New York City, but talking to him was like talking to that wall over there. He said, "We're moving," and we went to Suffolk, Virginia, around 1929. I was eight or nine at the time.

I still remember the smell of the South. It smelled like azaleas. And leaves. And peanuts. Peanuts everywhere. Planters peanuts had their headquarters in Suffolk. Mr.

Obici ran it. He was a big deal in town. The big peanut man. He gave a lot of money out to people. He built a hospital. You could buy peanuts by the pound in Suffolk for nothing. There were farmers growing peanuts, hauling peanuts, making peanut oil, peanut butter, even peanut soap. They called the high school yearbook The Peanut. *They even had a contest once to see who could make the best logo for Planters peanut company. Some lady won it. They gave her twenty-five dollars, which was a ton of money in those days.*

Suffolk was a one-horse town back then, one big Main Street, a couple of movie theaters—one for black folks, one for white folks—a few stores, a few farms nearby, and a set of railroad tracks that divided the black and white sections of town. The biggest event Suffolk had seen in years was a traveling sideshow that came through town on the railroad tracks, with a stuffed whale in a boxcar. The folks loved that. They loved anything different, or new, or from out of town, except for Jews. In school the kids called me "Christ killer" and "Jew baby." That name stuck with me for a long time. "Jew baby." You know it's so easy to hurt a child.

Tateh worked at the local synagogue, but he had his eye on this huge old barn-type building across the tracks on the so-called colored side of town with the aim of starting a grocery store there. Well, that upset some of the synagogue folks. They didn't want their holy rabbi going into business—and doing business with niggers, no less!—but Tateh said, "We're not moving anymore. I'm tired of moving." He knew they'd get rid of him eventually—let's face it, he was a lousy rabbi. He had a Jewish friend in town named Israel Levy who signed a bank note that allowed Tateh to get his hands on that old place. Tateh threw a counter and some shelves in there, an old cash register, tacked up a sign outside that said "Shilsky's Grocery Store" or something to that effect, and we were in business. The black folks called it "Old Man Shilsky's store." That's what they called him. Old Man Shilsky. They used to laugh at him and his old ragtag store behind his back, but over the years they made Old Man Shilsky rich and nobody was laughing then.

Our store was a rickety, odd, huge wooden structure that looked like it was held together with toothpicks and glue. It sat at the very edge of town, near the town jail and overlooking the wharf. On the first floor was the store, a storage area, an ice room, a kitchen with a kerosene stove, and the backyard. We slept upstairs. There was no living room, no dining room upstairs, just rooms. Me and Dee-Dee slept in one room under our big quilt. Mameh often slept in the same room as us, and my brother Sam and Tateh slept in the other. My parents didn't have the kind of warm relations that most parents had. Mameh was a very good wife and mother. Despite her overall poor health—she could barely see out of one eye, had severe pains in her stomach that grew more and more painful over the years—she could do more with one hand than I can do with two. She cooked matzoh balls, kneydlach, gefilte fish, kugl, chopped liver, and more kosher dishes than I can remember. She would darn socks. I learned how to chop fish, meat, and vegetables on a butcher-block cutting board from her. She kept the religious traditions of a Jewish housewife and was loyal to her husband, but Tateh had absolutely no love for her. He would call her by any name and make fun of her disability. He'd say, "I get sick to look at you," and, "Why do you bother trying to look pretty?" His marriage was a business deal for him. He only wanted money. That and to be an American. Those were the two things he wanted, and he got them too, but it cost him his family, which he ran into the ground and destroyed.

We had no family life. That store was our life. We worked in there from morning till night, except for school, and Tateh had us timed for that. He'd be standing in the road outside the store with his hands on his hips at three P.M. sharp, looking down the road for me and Sam, and later Dee-Dee, as we ran the six blocks home from school. Right to work we went. Homework was done between customers. We were the only store open in town on Sundays, because we celebrated our Sabbath from Friday to Saturday evening, so we did booming business on Sundays because the white folks would shop there as well as our normal customers.

We sold everything in that store: cigarettes, by the pack or loose—Camels, Lucky Strike, Chesterfields for a penny each, or Wings, two for a penny; we sold coal, lumber, firewood, kerosene, candy, Coca-Cola, BC powder, milk, cream, fruit, butter, canned goods, meat. Ice was a big product. It was put into the big wooden icebox in the back of the store and sold by the chunk or into smaller pieces that sold for fifteen cents each. That icebox was big enough for a person to walk in, which I never did. Anything that could close behind me, or trap me, I never liked. I'm claustrophobic. I can't stand feeling stuck or trapped in a place. I like to move. Even as a tiny girl I was like that. Hobbies? I had none. Running. That was my hobby. Sometimes when Tateh wasn't home, I'd tear out the door of the store and run. Just run anyplace. I would run down the back roads where the black folks lived, across the tracks to where the white folks were. I loved to sprint, just to feel the wind blowing on my face and see things and not be at home. I was always a running-type person.

Of course I had something to run from. My father did things to me when I was a young girl that I couldn't tell anyone about. Such as getting in bed with me at night and doing things to me sexually that I could not tell anyone about. When we'd go to the beach in Portsmouth, he'd get into the water with me, supposedly to teach me how to swim, and hold me real close to his body near his sexual parts and he'd have an erection. When we'd get back to the beach, Mameh would ask, "Are you getting better at swimming?" and I'd say, "Yes, Mameh," and he'd be standing there, glaring at me. God, I was scared of him.

Anytime he had a chance, he'd try to get close to me or crawl into bed with me and molest me. I was afraid of Tateh and had no love for him at all. I dreaded him and was relieved anytime he left the house. But it affected me in a lot of ways, what he did to me. I had very low self-esteem as a child, which I kept with me for many, many years; and even now I don't want to be around anyone who is domineering or pushing me around because it makes me nervous. I'm only telling you this because you're my son and I want you to know the truth and nothing less. I did have low self-esteem as a child. I felt low.

Folks will run with that, won't they? They'll say, "Oh, she felt low, so she went on and married a nigger." Well, I don't care. Your father changed my life. He taught me about a God who lifted me up and forgave me and made me new. I was lucky to meet him or I would've been a prostitute or dead. Who knows what would've happened to me. I was reborn in Christ. Had to be, after what I went through. Of course it wasn't torment twenty-four hours a day being a Jew. We had good times, especially with my mother. Like on Passover, where you had to clean that house spic-and-span. Not a crumb or speck of leavened bread could be found anywhere. We loved getting ready for it. You had to use Passover dishes and we had a big seder, where the family sat down and the table was set with matzoh and parsley, boiled eggs and other traditional Jewish food. We set an empty chair for the coming of Elijah—see, Jews think the real Messiah hasn't got here yet. The Haggadah had to be read and Tateh would ask us children questions about why we celebrated the feast of Passover. Well, you can believe we knew the answer rather than get smacked across the face by him, but to be honest with you, I used to see that empty chair we left for Elijah at the table and wish I could be gone to wherever Elijah was, eating over somebody else's house where your father didn't crawl into bed with you at night, interrupting your dreams so you don't know if it's really him or just the same nightmare happening over and over again.

6.

The New Testament

Mommy loved God. She went to church each and every Sunday, the only white person in sight, butchering the lovely hymns with a singing voice that sounded like a cross between a cold engine trying to crank on an October morning and a whining Maytag washer. My siblings and I would muffle our laughter as Mommy dug into hymns with verve and gusto: *"Leaning . . . oh, leannning . . . safe and secure on the—"* Up, up, and away she went, her shrill voice climbing higher and higher, reminding us of Curly of the Three Stooges. It sounded so horrible that I often thought Rev. Owens, our minister, would get up from his seat and stop the song. He'd sit behind his pulpit in a spiritual trance, his eyes closed, clad in a long blue robe with a white scarf and billowed sleeves, as if he were prepared to float away to heaven himself, until one of Mommy's clunker notes roused him. One eye would pop open with a jolt, as if someone had just poured cold water down his back. He'd coolly run the eye in a circle, gazing around at the congregation of forty-odd parishioners to see where the whirring noise was coming from. When his eye landed on Mommy, he'd nod as if to say, "Oh, it's just Sister Jordan"; then he'd slip back into his spiritual trance.

In the real world, Mommy was "Mrs. McBride" or "Mrs. Jordan," depending on whether she used my father's or stepfather's name, but in Rev. Owens's church, she was Sister Jordan. "Sister Jordan brought quite a few of her children today," Rev. Owens would marvel as Mommy stumbled in with six of us trailing her. "*Quite* a few." We thought he was hilarious. He was our Sunday school teacher and also the local barber who cut our hair once a month when we grew big enough to refuse Mommy's own efforts in that direction—she literally put a bowl on your head and cut around it. He was a thin man who wore polyester suits and styled his hair in the old slicked-back conk, combed to the back in rippling waves. He could not read very well—I could read better than he could when I was only twelve. He'd stand on the pulpit, handkerchief in hand, wrestling with the Bible verses like a man possessed. He'd begin with, "Our verse for today is . . . ahh, ummm, ahh . . ." flipping through the pages of his Bible, finally finding the verse, putting his finger on it, and you could hear the clock going *tick, tock, tick, tock,* as he struggled with the words, moving his lips silently while the church waited on edge and my sister Helen, the church pianist, stifled her giggles and Mommy glared at her, shaking her fist and silently promising vengeance once church was over.

Rev. Owens's sermons started like a tiny choo-choo train and ended up like a roaring locomotive. He'd begin in a slow drawl, then get warmed up and jerk back and forth over the subject matter like a stutterer gone wild: "We . . . [silence] . . . know . . . today . . . arrhh . . . um . . . I said WEEEE . . . know . . . THAT [silence] ahhh . . . JESUS [church: "Amen!"] . . . ahhh, CAME DOWN . . . ["Yes! Amen!"] I said CAME DOWWWWNNNN! ["Go on!"] He CAME - ON - DOWN - AND - LED - THE - PEOPLE - OF - JERU-SALEM- AMEN!" Then he'd shift to a babbling "Amen" mode, where he spoke in fast motion and the words popped out of his mouth like artillery rounds. "Amens" fired across the room like bullets. "It's so good AMEN to know God AMEN and I tell you AMEN that if you AMEN only come AMEN to God yourself AMEN there will be AMEN no turning back AMEN AMEN AMEN! Can I get an AMEN?" ("AMEN!")

And there we were in aisle 5, Sister Jordan in her church hat and blue dress, chuckling and smiling and occasionally waving her hands in the air like everyone else. Mommy loved church. Any church. Even Rev. Owens's Whosoever Baptist Church she loved, though he wasn't her favorite minister because he left his wife, or vice versa—we never knew. Mommy was a connoisseur of ministers; she knew them the way a French wine connoisseur knows Beaujolais red from Vouvray white. Rev. Owens, despite his preaching talents, wasn't even in the top five. That elite list included my late father, the late Rev. W. Abner Brown of Metropolitan Baptist in Harlem, our family friend Rev. Edward Belton, and a few others, all of whom were black, and with the exception of Rev. Belton, quite dead. She considered them old-timers, men of dignity and dedication who grew up in the South and remembered what life was like in the old days. They knew how to fire up a church the old-fashioned way, without talk of politics and bad mouthing and negativity but with real talk of God and genuine concern for its parishioners. "Your father," she often mused, "he'd give anybody his last dime." She did not like large churches with political preachers, nor Pentecostal churches that were too wild. And despite her slight dislike of Rev. Owens and his odd style—he once preached a sermon on the word "the"—T-H-E—she had respect for him because his church and preachings were close in style to that of her "home" church, New Brown Memorial. Unlike New Brown, however, Whosoever wasn't a storefront church. It was a tiny brick building that stood alone, about fifteen feet back from the sidewalk, with a sign above the door that was done by a painter who began his lettering without taking into account how little space he had. It read: WHOSOEVER BAPTIST CHURCH."

I never saw Mommy "get happy" at Whosoever Baptist, meaning "get the spirit" and lose control—thank God. When people got happy it was too much for me. They were mostly women, big mamas whom I knew and loved, but when the good Lord climbed into their bones and lifted them up toward Sweet Liberty, kind, gentle women who mussed my hair and kissed me on my cheek and gave me dimes would burst out of their seats like Pittsburgh Steeler linebackers. "Oh yessss!" they'd cry, arms outstretched, dancing in the aisles, slithering around with the agility of the Pink Panther, shuddering violently, purse flying one way, hat going another, while some poor old sober-looking deacon tried grimly to hang on to them to keep them from hurting themselves, only to be shaken off like a fly. Sometimes two or three people would physically hold the spirited person to keep her from hurting herself while we looked on in awe, the person convulsing and hollering, "Jesus, Jesus! Yes!" with Rev. Owens winging along with his spirited "AMEN'S" and "ah yes's!" I never understood why God would climb into these people with such fervor, until I became a grown man myself and came to understand the nature and power of God's many blessings, but even as a boy I knew God was all-powerful because of Mommy's utter deference to Him, and also because she would occasionally do something in church that I never saw her do at home or anywhere else: at some point in the service, usually when the congregation was singing one of her favorite songs, like "We've Come This Far by Faith" or "What a Friend We Have in Jesus," she would bow down her head and weep. It was the only time I ever saw her cry. "Why do you cry in church?" I asked her one afternoon after service.

"Because God makes me happy."

"Then why cry?"

"I'm crying 'cause I'm happy. Anything wrong with that?"

"No," I said, but there was, because happy people did not seem to cry like she did. Mommy's tears seemed to come from somewhere else, a place far away, a place inside her that she never let any of us children visit, and even as a boy I felt there was pain behind them. I thought it was because she wanted to be black like everyone else in church, because maybe God liked black people better, and one afternoon on the way home from church I asked her whether God was black or white.

A deep sigh. "Oh boy . . . God's not black. He's not white. He's a spirit."

"Does he like black or white people better?"

"He loves all people. He's a spirit."

"What's a spirit?"

"A spirit's a spirit."

"What color is God's spirit?"

"It doesn't have a color," she said. "God is the color of water. Water doesn't have a color."

I could buy that, and as I got older I still bought it, but my older brother Richie, who was the brother above me and the guy from whom I took all my cues, did not. When Richie was fourteen he'd grown from a tittering, cackling torturer of me to a handsome, slick high school kid who was an outstanding tenor sax player. He got accepted at Music and Art High School in Manhattan and had reached a point in his life where jazz was the beginning, the end, and the middle. He took to wearing a leather jacket and a porkpie hat like legendary tenor man Lester Young, joined a neighborhood R&B band, and Ma had increasing difficulty in getting him to go to school. The dudes in the neighborhood called him "Hatt" and respected him. The girls loved him. He was bursting with creative talent and had ideas he acted upon independently without the approval of, or the knowledge of, Ma. A few blocks from our house was an eight-foot-high stone with a plaque on it that commemorated some civil historic event, and one morning on the way to the store, Mommy noticed that the rock had been painted the black-liberation colors, red, black, and green. "I wonder who did that," she remarked. I knew, but I couldn't say. Richie had done it.

All my siblings, myself included, had some sort of color confusion at one time or another, but Richie dealt with his in a unique way. As a boy, he believed he was neither black nor white but rather green like the comic book character the Incredible Hulk. He made up games about it and absorbed the character completely into his daily life: "I'm Dr. Bruce Banner," he'd say as he saw me eating the last of the bologna and cheese. "I need a piece of your sandwich. Please give it to me now or I'll get angry. I must have it! Please don't make me angry. Give me *that sandwich!!!* GIVE ME—Oh no! Wait . . . ARRHHHHHHGGG-HHHH!" and thereby he'd become the Hulk and if I hadn't gobbled my sandwich by then, well, the Hulk got it.

One morning in Sunday school Richie raised his hand and asked Rev. Owens, "Is Jesus white?"

Rev. Owens said no.

"Then how come they make him white here in this picture?" Richie said, and he held up our Sunday school Bible.

Rev. Owens said, "Jesus is all colors."

"Then why is he white? This looks like a white man to me." Richie held the picture high so everyone in the class could see it. "Don't he look white to you?" Nobody said anything.

Rev. Owens was stuck. He stood there, wiping his face with his handkerchief and making the same noise he made when he preached. "Welllll . . . ahh. Welllll . . . ahhh . . ."

I was embarrassed. The rest of the kids stared at Richie like he was crazy. "Richie, forget it," I mumbled.

"Naw. If they put Jesus in this picture here, and He ain't white, and He ain't black, they should make Him gray. Jesus should be gray."

Richie stopped going to Sunday school after that, though he never stopped believing in God. Mommy tried and tried to make him go back, but he wouldn't.

Mommy took great pride in our relationship to God. Every Easter we had to perform at the New Brown Church, playing our instruments or reciting a story from the Bible for the entire church congregation. Mommy looked forward to this day with anticipation, while my siblings and I dreaded it like the plague, always waiting till the morning of the event before memorizing the Bible story we would recite. I never had problems with these memory-crunching sessions, but one year my older brother Billy, whose memory would later serve him well enough to take him through Yale University Medical School, marched to the front of the church wearing suit and tie, faced the congregation, started out, "When Jesus first came to . . ." then blanked out completely. He stood there, twitching nervously, dead in the water, while my siblings and I winced and held our breath to keep from laughing.

"Oh, that's all right now . . ." murmured my godfather, Deacon McNair, from his seat on the dais next to the minister, while Mommy twitched in her seat watching Billy, her face reddening. "Try it again," he said.

"Okay," Billy said, swallowing. "When Jesus first came to . . . No, wait. . . . Um. Jerusalem was . . . Wait a minute. . . ." He stood there, stalled, gazing at the ceiling, biting his lip, desperately trying to remember the Bible story he had memorized just a half hour before, while the church murmured, "Oh it's all right now . . . just keep trying," and Mommy glared at him, furious.

A few more embarrassing seconds passed. Finally Deacon McNair said, "Well, you don't have to tell us a Bible story, Billy. Just recite a verse from the Bible."

"Any verse?" Billy asked.

"Any verse you want," the deacon said.

"Okay." Billy faced the church again. Every face was silent, watching him.

"Jesus wept," he said. He took his seat.

Dead silence.

"Amen," said Deacon McNair.

After church, we followed Mommy as she stalked out, and my godfather met her at the door. "It's all right, Ruth," he said, chuckling.

"No it's not," Ma said.

When we got home, Mommy beat Billy's butt.

7.

Sam

Our store was at an intersection at the edge of town on a long, sloping hill. If you stood in front of the store and looked right, you saw the town—the railroad tracks, the department stores like Leggets and Woolworth. If you looked straight ahead, you saw the courthouse, the jailhouse, the county clerk's office, and the road to Norfolk. To the left was the Jaffe slaughterhouse and the wharf where the Nansemond River met the Main Street Bridge. The wharf was huge and dark. Boats from all over the world would stop there to lay over or make repairs, and often the sailors would come into the store and invite me and my sister Dee-Dee to see their boats. "No, no thank you," my mother would say. She couldn't understand a word they were saying, but as soon as they'd say, "Come with us," she'd hop out of her chair by the door and stand in front of those big sailors shaking her head. "No, no, go away. Tell them to go away," she'd say in Yiddish. She'd never take her eyes off them.

We were right at the intersection where the road from Norfolk and Portsmouth came into Suffolk. That intersection always had a lot of traffic on it. I don't mean traffic like you see today. In those days, two or three cars was traffic. Or people on foot. Or farmers leading mules hauling peanut crops on a wagon. Or soldiers on trucks from the bases in Norfolk. Or men in chain gangs. People got about any way they could in those days.

I was sitting behind the counter of the store one afternoon and a car full of men wearing white sheets drove past. They had white hats covering their faces, with two little eyeholes cut out so they could see. They were driving those old black tin lizzie–type cars, the Model A types, with two men in the open section up front and two in the cab section behind. Car after car of them drove by, so many it was like a parade. We came from behind the counter and stood outside the store to look at them. "What the heck is that?" Dee-Dee asked. "I don't know," I said.

That was the Ku Klux Klan riding through.

I didn't know the Ku Klux Klan from Cracker Jacks, but our black customers slipped out and dashed into their homes as soon as they caught sight of them. They kept out of sight and low key, very low key when the Klan showed up. The Klan would ride right up Main Street in broad daylight and no one did a thing about it. It seemed to me death was always around Suffolk. I was always hearing about somebody found hanged or floating in the wharf. And we were uneasy too, my family, because in the South there was always a lot of liquor and drinking, and Jews weren't popular. Tateh kept a loaded pistol underneath the counter next to the cashier. He cleaned that gun more than he cleaned his own trousers, and he had it ready for anyone who tried to fool with his money. He trusted no one. He thought black folks were always trying to steal from him. He'd sit my mother next to the door and say in Yiddish, "Watch the shvartses." He was robbing these folks blind, charging them a hundred percent markup on his cheap goods, and he was worried about them stealing from him!

I was always worried that Tateh's gun would go off and accidentally kill him *while he was cleaning it. Although I was afraid of him, I didn't want anything to happen to him. We had a neighbor, Mrs. Brown, a white woman who had a puffed-up middle finger from some infection she had gotten——in those days, folks got infections and lost their fingers and teeth like it was lunch. In fact, my mother and father both had false teeth. My mother got 'em first, and later ol' Tateh, he snuck off and got him a pair. He barked an order at me one day, something like, "Pick up those soap bars," and I looked in his mouth and saw a brand-new set of white chompers. I said to myself, "I knew he was sounding funny." Anyhow, Mrs. Brown was one of the few white folks in Suffolk that was nice to me. She had a daughter named Marilyn and a son named Simon. Simon was an alcoholic who used to come teetering home at night. He got killed by a drunk who climbed onto his porch and drove a knife down his neck. Marilyn, she worked downtown and her boss was cleaning his pistol in his office and accidentally shot himself to death, and Marilyn had to step over his body to get out of there. That shook her up bad, and it shook me up too, because Tateh was always cleaning his gun, and if it went off and accidentally killed him I sure wasn't gonna step over his body to get out. I'd jump out the window first and he'd have to lay there and gather flies till somebody else got him. I never did like dead people and I never did like guns. That's why I never let my children play with toy guns.*

But in those days, people used guns to hunt and live. This was the thirties, the depression, and folks were poor and they used guns and fishing rods to survive. If you got sick, God help you because you just died. Tuberculosis and double pneumonia were raging in those days, and Mameh had a great fear one of her kids would catch that, because in Europe one of her brothers died in a flu epidemic. But after we got that store going we made money and could afford a doctor. Black folks, our customers, they'd come into the store and buy BC powder, fill up on that, that was their doctor. That was the old powder you bought and took like aspirin. It was a brand name. BC powder. It cost twenty-five cents and came in a little blue-and-white packet. Folks said it made them feel better and pepped them up. Of course it had cocaine in it back then, but folks didn't know that. They'd take BC for any ailment. In fact, if somebody came in buying too much of it for his wife or child, you got concerned, because somebody tak-

ing that much BC was mighty sick and probably dying. Folks got sick and died back in them days like it was a new dance coming out. Plop! Dead as a doornail.

I wish some of these black kids today could see how the black folks in Suffolk lived then. Lord, you wouldn't believe it. Shacks with no running water, no foundations, no bathrooms, outhouses. No paved roads, no electricity. Sometimes Mameh and I would walk down those dirt roads behind the store and so many of those roads dead-ended into woods. That's how life was for blacks down there. A dead end.

They didn't complain about it. Who would they complain to? The cops? The cops wouldn't ride back there, you crazy? They were scared to or didn't want to. But what always struck me about black folks was that every Sunday they'd get dressed up so clean for church I wouldn't recognize them. I liked that. They seemed to have such a purpose come Sunday morning. Their families were together and although they were poor, they seemed happy. Tateh hated black people. He'd call the little children bad names in Yiddish and make fun of their parents, too. "Look at them laughing," he'd say in Yiddish. "They don't have a dime in their pocket and they're always laughing." But he had plenty money and we were all miserable. My brother Sam, he couldn't take it and ran off as soon as he got big enough.

Sam was like a shadow. He was short and stocky, with a heavy head of hair, thick eyebrows, and heavy arms and legs. Because he was two years older than me, he had plenty power over me and Dee-Dee, yet he didn't use his older-brother status over us. He was quiet and submissive. Mameh doted on him, but Tateh put the fear of God into him. Every evening after supper Tateh would sit me and Sam down and make us study the Old Testament. Dee-Dee was too young for that, but me and Sam weren't. He'd read the words to us and make us repeat them back to him. The book of Ecclesiastes was Tateh's favorite. "I said in my heart, God shall judge the righteous and the wicked; for there is a time for every purpose and every work." That's Ecclesiastes. I still know those verses, but I learned them out of . . . not out of love for God but just out of . . . what? . . . I don't know. Duty. My father was a rabbi, right? Shouldn't his kids know the Old Testament? We hated those sessions. Tateh had no patience, and he'd often stop you in the middle of your verse to scold or slap you if you showed disinterest in the Bible. Sometimes the scolding made you feel worse than the hitting. "You're stupid. You're nothing but a fool. A sinner. You're unredeemed before God," he'd say. Sam was his main target. He'd make Sam sit in the corner for hours and read Hebrew. He never showed any love toward his son.

You know, any rabbi who visited town, we'd have to put him up and feed him. Tateh would say, "You go show such and such around town," and we'd have to drag this old rabbi, some old fart, around and do what he told us. We hated that. Of course the alternative was Tateh would pull his belt off and skin you alive.

I liked to play dominoes with Sam when we were little, but as he got bigger, he had no time to play. Tateh worked Sam harder than me and Dee-Dee. Sam worked like a man when he was a boy. We'd open up the store at seven A.M., and Sam would saw lumber, cut ice, stack the meats out, stock the shelves, feed the cow in the backyard, all before we left for school. He hated that store. After school he went right to work. When he wanted to get out of working in the store, he wouldn't show up after school until almost dark, and Tateh would scold and punish him by making him work even longer hours. Sam had poor grades in school and low self-esteem from all that treatment. He had few friends because he was shy, and even if he did make a friend, we weren't allowed to have gentile friends. That was forbidden, aveyre.

He got bar mitzvahed when he was thirteen. They put a picture of him and Tateh in the paper and Mameh was proud of him. That was the only time I ever remember seeing him smile, because he made his mother happy. Then a couple of years later he ran off. This was around 1934. He just left home and never came back. He was about fifteen or so. He went to Chicago and wrote Mameh a letter from there. The letter was written in English, which Mameh didn't read or speak, but I read it for her. It said, "I am fine. I got a job working as a clerk in a store." He got a job working for Montgomery Ward or J. C. Penney, one of those stores. He didn't know a soul in Chicago and made it there on his own. Mameh was beside herself with that letter. "Write him back," she told me. "Write him back now and tell him to come home." So I did. I wrote Sam and told him to come home, but he never did come home and I never did see him again.

He joined the army and got killed in World War II, my brother Sam. I didn't find out what happened to him till long after the fact, when your daddy died in 1957. I had seven kids and was pregnant with you and I called one of my aunts to ask for help and she said, "Your brother died in the war." I asked her what happened, and she said, "Stay out of our lives. You've been out. Stay out." And she hung up on me, so there was nothing I could do for Sam but pray for him.

8.

Brothers and Sisters

Mommy's house was orchestrated chaos and as the eighth of twelve children, I was lost in the sauce, so to speak. I was neither the prettiest, nor the youngest, nor the brightest. In a house where there was little money and little food, your power was derived from who you could order around. I was what Mommy called a "Little Kid," one of five young'uns, microscopic dots on the power grid of the household, thus fit to be tied, tortured, tickled, tormented, ignored, and commanded to suffer all sorts of indignities at the hands of the "Big Kids," who didn't have to go to bed early, didn't believe in the tooth fairy, and were appointed denizens of power by Mommy, who of course wielded ultimate power.

My brothers and sisters were my best friends, but when it came to food, they were my enemies. There were so many of us we were constantly hungry, scavenging for food in the empty refrigerator and cabinets. We would hide food from one another, squirreling away a precious grilled cheese or fried bologna sandwich, but the hiding places were known to all and foraged by all and the precious commodity was usually discovered and devoured before it got cold. Entire plots were hatched around swiping food, complete with double-crossing, backstabbing, intrigue, outright robbery, and gobbled evidence. Back in the projects in Red Hook, before we moved to Queens, Mommy would disappear in the morning and return later with huge cans of peanut butter which some benevolent agency had distributed from some basement area in the housing projects. We'd gather around the cans, open them, and spoon up the peanut butter like soup, giggling as our mouths stuck closed with the gooey stuff. When Mommy left for work, we dipped white bread in syrup for lunch, or ate brown sugar raw out of the box, which was a good hunger killer. We had a toaster that shocked you every time you touched it; we called our toast *shock*toast and we got shocked so much our hair stood on end like Buckwheat's. Ma often lamented the fact that she could not afford to buy us fruit, sometimes for weeks at a time, but we didn't mind. We spent every penny we had on junk food. "If you eat that stuff your teeth will drop out," Mommy warned. We ignored her. "If you chew gum and swallow it, your behind will close up," she said. We listened and never swallowed gum. We learned to eat standing up, sitting down, lying down, and half asleep, because there were never enough places at the table for everyone to sit, and there was always a mad scramble for Ma's purse when she showed up at two A.M. from work. The cafeteria at the Chase Manhattan Bank where she worked served dinner to the employees for free, so she would load up with bologna sandwiches, cheese, cakes, whatever she could pillage, and bring it home for the hordes to devour. If you were the first to grab the purse when she got home, you ate. If you missed it, well, sleep tight.

The food she brought from work was delicious, particularly when compared to the food she cooked. Mommy could not cook to save her life. Her grits tasted like sand and butter, with big lumps inside that caught in your teeth and stuck in your gums. Her pancakes had white goo and egg shells in them. Her stew would send my little brother Henry upstairs in disgust. "Prison stew," he'd sniff, coming back a few minutes later to help himself before the masses devoured it. She had little time to cook anyway. When she got home from work she was exhausted. We'd come downstairs in the morning to find her still dressed and fast asleep at the kitchen table, her head resting on the pages of someone's homework, a cold cup of coffee next to her sleeping head. Her housework rivaled her cooking. "I'm the worst housekeeper I've ever seen," she declared, and that was no lie. Our house looked like a hurricane hit it. Books, papers, shoes, football helmets, baseball bats, dolls, trucks, bicycles, musical instruments, lay everywhere and were used by everyone. All the boys slept in one room, girls slept in another, but the labels "boys' room" and "girls' room" meant nothing. We snuck into each other's rooms by night to trade secrets, argue, commiserate, spy, and continue chess games and monopoly games that had begun days earlier. Four of us played the same clarinet, handing it off to one another in the hallway at school like halfbacks on a football field. Same with coats, hats, sneakers, clean socks, and gym uniforms. One washcloth was used by all. A solitary toothbrush would cover five sets of teeth and gums. We all swore it belonged to us personally. Our furniture consisted of two beautiful rocking chairs that Ma bought from Macy's because on television she saw her hero President John F. Kennedy use one to rock his kids, a living room couch, and an assortment of chairs, tables, dressers, and beds. The old black-and-white TV set worked—sometimes. It wasn't high on Mommy's list of things to fix. She called it "the boob tube" and rarely allowed us to watch it. We didn't need to.

Our house was a combination three-ring circus and zoo, complete with ongoing action, daring feats, music, and animals. Over the years we assembled a stable of pets that resembled a veritable petting zoo: gerbils, mice, dogs, cats, rabbits, fish, birds, turtles, and frogs that would alternatively lick and bite us and spread mysterious diseases that zipped through our house as if it were a Third World country, prompting health clinic visits chaperoned by Ma where bored doctors slammed needles into our butts like we were on a GMC assembly line. Ma once brought home a chick for Easter, and it grew and grew until she came home from work one night, opened the door, and saw eight kids chasing a rooster around the living room. "Get him out!" she screamed. He was removed and eventually replaced by a fierce German shepherd named Abe who bit us all and would occasionally leave a mound of dog poop in a corner somewhere, then growl and dare us to beat him for it. The mound would sit, untouched. After a day the odor would dissipate and we'd avoid it further until it dried up and hardened like a rock, whereupon some brave soul would kick the offending artifact under the radiator, where it would fester and further fossilize into dust or extinction or discovery.

We never consulted Mommy about these problems. Her time merited only full-blown problems like, "Is the kitchen floor still under two feet of water since y'all flooded it?" and school, which was a top priority. Excuses for not doing homework were not accepted and would draw a beating. Cursing was not allowed. We weren't even allowed to say the word "lie," we had to use "story." "Do your homework and don't tell stories and you might become like your brother

Dennis," Mommy admonished. "Just look at how good he's doing. Educate your mind like your brother *Dennis.*"

Dennis.

You could hear the sighs all through the house when she mentioned that name. They sounded like the whistle on the Long Island Rail Road that passed by on the tracks a few blocks from our house.

Dennis was the eldest sibling and the family pioneer. He was an artist who drew pictures that told incredible stories about the places he'd been and the people he'd met. He had money in his pocket, actual dollars and cents, with change to spare. He was a giant among us, casting a huge, oblong shadow that hung over us children like the Lincoln Memorial, which he had visited—twice. His great achievements, spoken of in his absence because he came home only for holidays, were glowingly recounted, dissected, rumored, enhanced, extolled. The heights he had attained, heights we puny mortals could only dream of achieving, were trumpeted and crowed about by Mommy in every corner of the house. Dennis had finished college. Dennis had gone to Europe. And now, for his crowning achievement, Dennis, oh glorious Dennis, oh mighty Dennis—Dennis! *Dennis!*—sought the highest, most wonderful, most incredible achievement any human being, any son, could hope to achieve.

Dennis was going to be a doctor.

Well, there was no greater honor. I mean, forget it. Doctor, teacher, take your pick. Had Mommy known what Dennis was really doing in school, other than being a straight-A student, she might have had a different opinion of him. Dennis was one of the most active civil rights students the University of Pennsylvania Medical School had ever seen. He marched on Washington. He organized a hospital workers' union. He sat in at lunch counters in the South. He got sprayed with Mace and fire-hosed by civil authorities. Dennis was at war with the system, but as long as he kept his war out of the house and stayed in medical school, that was okay with Mommy. But my sister Helen didn't do that. Helen was at war with the white man and took it home and laid it at Mommy's feet.

Helen was the second-eldest of my sisters, all of whom were gentle, naive, talkative, and curious, which is why Mommy kept them off the street and away from men at all times. They were all pretty, ranging from Helen's deep brown skin to Kathy's very light, almost white skin, and all had long arms, freckles, and dark curly hair. Every boy in my neighborhood knew my five sisters by name and face. I would walk down the street and some big dude I'd never seen before would say, "Yo. How's Kathy?" "Okay," I'd shrug. I got my nose nearly broken over Kathy a few times. There's nothing worse than having to fight for your crummy, ugly sister whom half the neighborhood is in love with. It was a real problem.

Helen was the most artistic of my sisters. She was slim, with black hair that she wore in a bun, jeans, and a denim jacket with peace insignias, "Stop the War" buttons, and red, black, and green liberation patches sewn on. Boys of all types—black, white, Asian, Latino—followed her everywhere. She was a student at Music and Art High School, and played piano for our church choir until, one Sunday morning, my youngest sister Judy, who was nine and also played piano, was suddenly pressed into service. It seemed that Helen had retired from playing for church that morning. When Mommy asked why, Helen said, "I don't want to," and that was the end of it. Such terse responses to Mommy were unheard of. We watched in awe as Helen stood her ground, repeated her resolve not to play for the church choir, and survived a beating with the belt by Mommy without a whimper. She shrugged when Mommy was done.

Not too long afterwards, the dean of Music and Art called our house and asked Ma why Helen was quitting school. "You must be joking," Ma said. "All my kids are A students."

"Not this one," the dean said. "She quit two weeks ago. It's a shame," he said.

Mommy beat Helen harder this time, then talked to her for hours. Helen cried after the beating, promised to change after the talks, then shrugged and kept on missing school. Mommy enrolled her in two more schools, but she quit both, declaring, "The white man's education is not for me." She became a complete hippie before our astonished eyes, dressing in beads and berets and wearing sweet-smelling oils that, she said, gave you certain powers. A folk guitar player named Eric Bibb followed her everywhere. We were awed. Mommy called in reinforcements—ministers, friends, my stepfather—but Helen ignored them. She sat up late at night with my elder siblings and talked about the revolution against the white man while we Little Kids slept upstairs. My little sister Kathy and I would creep to the top of the stairs in our underwear, listening as the Big Kids had animated conversations about "changing the system" and "the revolution," extolling the virtues of Martin Luther King over Malcolm X and vice versa, and playing records by the Last Poets. Helen, once a peripheral figure in these discussions, became the epicenter, instigator, and protagonist. "You have to fight the system!" she'd yell. "Fight the Man!"

This would set off a barrage of laughing commentary from my elder siblings, gurus of life and wisdom who had seen and done it all.

"Yes, but is the Man you? Or are you the Man?"

"Do you mean the *Man*, or the *Wo*-man!"

"Who is the Man . . . ?"

"But are you the *Main* Man . . . ?"

(Sung) *"When a maaan loves a wooomannnn!!"*

These goof sessions, which almost always ended as earnest talks on civil rights, often went on until Mommy got home from work.

One night as Kathy and I lay upstairs pretending to be asleep—we sometimes snuck over to each other's rooms—we heard a tremendous *boom!* followed by cursing and swearing. We sat straight up. Downstairs, Helen and Rosetta were having a fight.

It was not often that my siblings had true fights, but when they did, they were monster, one-on-one fisticuff affairs, and Helen had picked the Mount Everest of fighters. Rosetta was the eldest sister and the smartest of all my siblings. From her perch atop her bed—a bed, incidentally, that she shared with no one—Rosetta sat regally on a throne of bed pillows, legs crossed Buddha fashion, while drinking ice water, listening to her favorite public radio station, WBAI, and giving commands all day. She would order us to serve her ice water in tall glasses and send us to the candy store for Devil Dogs and Montclair cigarettes, which we fetched with great dispatch and offered to her with proper subservience. She slept with the radio blasting and the lights on. While she napped, we would creep past her bed, afraid to arouse the slumbering master. She defied anyone to challenge her. My older brothers wore their hats sideways and talked in low voices about Jim Brown and Muhammad Ali, but not even the boldest of them, not even eldest brother Dennis, to whom we all bowed low, fooled with Rosetta. Rosetta was the resident queen of the house.

I heard the sound of a coat tearing. *Rrrrrrip!*

"You bitch!" Helen screamed. I heard fists landing on flesh. Rosetta roared.

Kathy started to cry. "Be quiet," I said. Cursing in my house was not allowed. Cursing was out of bounds. Cursing meant things were out of control.

More commotion. I heard the boys downstairs saying, "All right, break it up. Hold her, Billy, wait—" *Boom!* Laughter by the boys, an agonized cry by Rosetta. "Oh, you're gonna get it now!" *Whomp!* Helen's scream. Another tussle. The sound of furniture flying, David shouting, a lamp breaking. More laughter and cursing . . . A vehement argument ensued, and I heard Helen declare she was leaving. Suddenly the boys got serious.

"Wait a minute!"

"Hold up! Hold up!"

"This is crazy!"

"Don't touch me," Helen said. "Don't nobody touch me. Y'all make me sick. Every single one of you."

Titters and giggles.

"I'm sick of this house!"

Silence. A sob. Then heavy weeping.

"Aw . . . Helen . . ."

I heard the sound of the door opening, then slamming shut.

Later that night, when Mommy came from work and saw all the lights on and all of us, even the Little Kids, downstairs waiting for her in the kitchen, she knew there was trouble. "Where's Helen?" she asked, panic climbing into her voice.

"Gone," she was told.

"Why did you let her go?" she asked.

"She wouldn't stay, Ma. We tried to make her stay but she wouldn't."

"Oh Lord . . ." Mommy moaned, slapping her forehead, then balling her fists. "Why didn't you make her stay? Why?" Silence, as we blinked and gulped, guilt settling on us like rain clouds.

Helen didn't come home that night. Nor the next day. Nor the next. She was fifteen years old. Mommy called the police the second day. They came and took a report. They searched the neighborhood, but couldn't find her. Mommy called all Helen's friends. Still no Helen. The following week my sister Jack called Mommy from her apartment in Harlem. Helen loved Jack. Everybody loved Jack. You could talk to Jack about anything. "Ruth, she's with me," Jack said. "She doesn't want to see you, but don't worry. Let it blow over. Don't scare her off." But Mommy couldn't wait. She hung up the phone and summoned my brother Richie to the kitchen, gave him carfare and explicit instructions: Tell Helen all is forgiven. Just come home.

Richie dutifully donned his leather coat, popped his Lester Young porkpie hat on his head, and headed for Harlem while Mommy paced the floor, on edge. He returned late that night with his hat pushed far back on his forehead. "She's not comin' home, Ma," he said.

Shortly after, Helen left Jack's altogether and disappeared.

Mommy was beside herself. She spent entire nights pacing up and down the floor. She called on preachers and friends from church, called on my stepfather, who made several rare, during-the-week appearances. More solutions were discussed. Prayers were said. Regrets taken. Apologies made. But there was no Helen. "She'll come back," Daddy said. "It'll work out." He had no idea what to do about Helen. They spoke a completely different language. He was an old-timer who called school "schoolin' " and called me "boy." He had run off from Jim Crow in the South and felt that education, any education, was a privilege. Helen was far beyond that.

Weeks passed, months, and Helen didn't return.

Finally Jack called. "I found her. She's living with some crazy woman," Jack said. She told Ma she didn't know much about the lady other than that she wore a lot of scarves and used incense. Mommy got the address and went to the place herself.

It was a dilapidated housing project near St. Nicholas Avenue, with junkies and winos standing out front. Mommy stepped past them and walked through a haze of reefer smoke and took the elevator to the eighth floor. She went to the apartment door and listened. There was music playing on a stereo inside, and the voice of someone on the phone. She knocked on the door. The stereo lowered. "Who is it?" someone asked. It sounded like Helen.

"I'm here to see Helen," Mommy said.

Silence.

"I know you're there, Helen," Mommy said.

Silence.

"Helen. I want you to come home. Whatever's wrong we'll fix. Just forget all of it and come on home." From down the hallway, a doorway opened and a black woman watched in silence as the dark-haired, bowlegged white lady talked to the closed door.

"Please come home, Helen."

The door had a peephole in it. The peephole slid back. A large black eye peered out.

"Please come home, Helen. This is no place for you to be. Just come on home."

The peephole closed.

9.

Shul

In Suffolk, they had a white folks' school and a black folks' school and a Jewish school. You called the Jewish school "shul" in Yiddish. It wasn't really a school. It was just the synagogue where Tateh taught Hebrew lessons and gave Bible study to children and taught cantoring to boys and that sort of thing. He'd practice his singing around the house sometimes, singing "do re mi fa sol," and all that. You know, they'd let him circumcise children too. That was part of his job as a rabbi, to go to people's houses and circumcise their kids. He had special knives for it. He'd also kill cows in the kosher faith for the Jews in town to eat, and we often kept a cow in the yard behind the store. We'd lead the cow to the Jaffe slaughterhouse down the road and the butchers would tie it from the ceiling by its hind legs. Tateh would open his knife case—he had a special velvet case with knives just for this purpose—and carefully select one of those big, *shiny knives. Then he'd utter a quick prayer and plunge the knife blade into the cow's neck. The cow would shudder violently and blood would spurt down his neck and through his nose into a drain in the cement floor and he'd die. The butchers would then set upon him and slit his stomach and yank out his intestines, heart, liver, and innards.*

I was almost grown before I could eat meat. The sight of my father plunging his knife into that cow was enough to make me avoid it for years. I was terrified of my father. He put the fear of God in me.

The Jewish school didn't really count with the white folks, so I went to the white school, Thomas Jefferson Elementary. If it was up to Tateh he would have kept me out of school altogether. "That gentile school won't teach you anything you can use," he scoffed. He paid for us to take private lessons in sewing and knitting and record keeping from other people. He was tight with his money, but when it came to that kind of thing, he wasn't cheap, I'll say that for him. He would rather pay for us to study privately than to go to school with gentiles, but the law was the law, so I had to go to school with the white folks. It was a problem from the moment I started, because the white kids hated Jews in my school. "Hey, Ruth, when did you start being a dirty Jew?" they'd ask. I couldn't stand being ridiculed. I even changed my name to try to fit in more. My real name was Rachel, which in Yiddish is Ruckla, which is what my parents called me—but I used the name Ruth around white folk, because it didn't sound so Jewish, though it never stopped the other kids from teasing me.

Nobody liked me. That's how I felt as a child. I know what it feels like when people laugh at you walking down the street, or snicker when they hear you speaking Yiddish, or just look at you with hate in their eyes. You know a Jew living in Suffolk when I was coming up could be lonely even if there were fifteen of them standing in the room, I don't know why; it's that feeling that nobody likes you; that's how I felt, living in the South. You were different from everyone and liked by very few. There were white sections of Suffolk, like the Riverview section, where Jews weren't allowed to own property. It said that on the deeds and you can look them up. They'd say "for White Anglo-Saxon Protestants only." That was the law there and they meant it. The Jews in Suffolk did stick together, but even among Jews my family was low because we dealt with shvartses. So I didn't have a lot of Jewish friends either.

When I was in the fourth grade, a girl came up to me in the schoolyard during recess and said, "You have the prettiest hair. Let's be friends." I said, "Okay." Heck, I was glad someone wanted to be my friend. Her name was Frances. I'll never forget Frances for as long as I live. She was thin, with light brown hair and blue eyes. She was a quiet gentle person. I was actually forbidden to play with her because she was a gentile, but I'd sneak over to her house anyway and sneak her over to mine. Actually I didn't have to sneak into Frances's house because I was always welcome there. She lived past the cemetery on the other side of town in a frame house that we entered from the back door. It seemed that dinner was always being served at Frances's house. Her mother would serve it on plates she took out of a wooden china closet: ham, chicken, potatoes, corn, string beans, sliced tomatoes, lima beans, white bread, and hot biscuits with lots of butter—and I couldn't eat any of it. It was treyf, not kosher for a Jew to eat. The first time her mother served me dinner I said, "I can't eat this," and I was embarrassed until Frances piped out, "I don't like this food either. My favorite food is mayonnaise on white bread." That's how she was. She'd do little things to let you know she was on your side. It didn't bother her one bit that I was Jewish, and if she was around, no one in school would tease me.

I would take pennies from the store cash register so Frances and I could go to the Chadwick Movie Theater—it cost only ten cents. Or we would cut through the town cemetery on the way home from school so Tateh wouldn't see us; we'd spend a lot of afternoons sitting on the headstones talking. You know I'm spooked around dead folks. To this day you can't get me near a graveyard. But when I was with Frances, it didn't bother me a bit. It seemed like the easiest, most natural thing in world, to sit on somebody's headstone under the cool shade of a tree and chat. We always lingered till the last minute and when it was time to go, we'd have to run in separate directions to get home, so I'd watch her go first to make sure no ghosts were trying to catch her. She'd back away, facing me, asking, "Any ghosts behind me, Ruth? Is it clear?" I'd say, "Yeah. It's clear."

Then she'd turn around and scamper off, dodging the headstones and yelling over her shoulder, "You still watching, Ruth? Watch out for me!"

"I'm watching! No ghosts!" I'd shout. Then after a few seconds I'd yell, "I'm counting now!" I'd count to ten like this: "One two three four five . . . ten!"—and fly home! Fly through that cemetery!

Frances's family wasn't rich. They were like a lot of white folks back then. Farming-type folks, poor. Not poor like you see today. Back then it was a different kind of poor. A better kind of poor, but poor just the same. What I mean by that is you didn't need money as much, but you didn't have any neither. Just about everyone I knew was poor. A lot of our customers were so poor it wasn't funny. Black and white were poor. They got their food from the Nansemond River down the hill from our store. The men would go fishing and crabbing at the wharf and catch huge turtles and take them home and make soup and stew out of them. There was a man who all he did was haul in turtles. He'd walk home carrying a huge turtle under his arm the way you carry a schoolbook, and me and Dee-Dee would gawk. Sometimes he'd stop at the store and buy various ingredients for his turtle soup, various spices and garnishes. That turtle would still be alive, kicking and trying to get away while the man was standing in the store, poring over the vegetables, buying garlics and peppers to cook it up with. I used to feel sorry for the turtles. I wanted him to throw them back in the water, but I wouldn't say that. You crazy? Shoot! He wouldn't throw them back in the water for nobody. They were his dinner.

Folks were poor, and starving. And I have to admit I never starved like a lot of people did. I never had to eat turtles and crabs out of the wharf like a lot of folks did. I never starved for food till I got married. But I was starving in another way. I was starving for love and affection. I didn't get none of that.

10.

School

Back in the 1960s, when she had money, which was hardly ever, Mommy would take us down to Delancey Street on Manhattan's Lower East Side to shop for school clothes. "You have to go where the deals are," she said. "They won't come to you."

"Where are the deals?" we asked.

"The Jews have the deals."

I thought Jews were something that was in the Bible. I'd heard about them in Sunday school, through Jesus and such. I told Ma I didn't know they were still around.

"Oh, they're around," she said. She had a funny look on her face. The Hasidic Jewish merchants in their black yarmulkes would

65

stare in shock as Mommy walked in, trailed by five or six of us. When they recovered enough to make money, she would drive them to the wall, haggling them to death, lapsing into Yiddish when the going got tough. "I know what's happening here! I know what's happening!" she snapped when the merchants lapsed into Yiddish amongst themselves during negotiations over a pair of shoes. She angrily whipped off some gibberish and the merchants gawked even more. We were awed.

The first time it happened, we asked, "Ma, how'd you learn to talk like that?"

"Mind your own business," she said. "Never ask questions or your mind will end up like a rock. Some of these Jews can't stand you."

Looking back, I realize that I never felt any kinetic relationship to Jews. We were insulated from their world and any other world but our own. Yet there was a part of me that recognized Jews as slightly different from other white folks, partly through information gleaned from Mommy, who consciously and unconsciously sought many things Jewish, and partly through my elder siblings. My sister Rosetta's college education at the all-black Howard University was completely paid for—tuition, books, even school clothes—by the Joseph L. Fisher Foundation, which was run out of the Stephen Wise Free Synagogue of Manhattan. In addition, my oldest brother, Dennis, guru of wisdom and source of much of our worldly news in the 1960s, came home from college with respect for Jewish friends he'd met. "They support the civil rights movement," he reported. Mommy was for anything involving the improvement of our education and condition, and while she would be quick to point out that "some Jews can't stand you," she also, in her crazy contradictory way, communicated the sense to us that if we were lucky enough to come across the right Jew in our travels—a teacher, a cop, a merchant—he would be kinder than other white folks. She never spoke about Jewish people as white. She spoke about them as Jews, which made them somehow different. It was a feeling every single one of us took into adulthood, that Jews were different from white people somehow. Later as an adult when I heard folks talk of the love/hate relationship between blacks and Jews I understood it to the bone not because of any outside sociological study, but because of my own experience with Jewish teachers and classmates—some who were truly kind, genuine, and sensitive, others who could not hide their distaste for my black face—people I'd met during my own contacts with the Jewish world, which Mommy tacitly arranged by forcing every one of us to go to predominantly Jewish public schools.

It was in her sense of education, more than any other, that Mommy conveyed her Jewishness to us. She admired the way Jewish parents raised their children to be scholastic standouts, insulating them from a potentially harmful and dangerous public school system by clustering together within certain communities, to attend certain schools, to be taught by certain teachers who enforced discipline and encouraged learning, and she followed their lead. During the school year she gave us careful instructions to bring home every single paper that the teachers handed out at school, especially in January, and failure to follow these instructions resulted in severe beatings. When we dutifully arrived with the papers, she would pore over them carefully, searching—"Okay . . . okay . . . here it is!"—grabbing the little form and filling it out. Every year the mighty bureaucratic dinosaur known as the New York City Public School System would belch forth a tiny diamond: they slipped a little notice to parents giving them the opportunity to have their kids bused to different school districts if they wanted; but there was a limited time to enroll, a short window of opportunity that lasted only a few days. Mommy stood poised over that option like a hawk. She invariably chose predominantly Jewish public schools: P.S. 138 in Rosedale, J.H.S. 231 in Springfield Gardens, Benjamin Cardozo, Francis Lewis, Forest Hills, Music and Art. Every morning we hit the door at six-thirty, fanning out across the city like soldiers, armed with books, T squares, musical instruments, an "S" bus pass that allowed you to ride the bus and subway for a nickel, and a free-school-lunch coupon in our pocket. Even the tiniest of us knew the subway and local city bus schedules and routes by heart. *The number 3 bus lets you off at the corner, but the 3A turns, so you have to get off . . .* By age twelve, I was traveling an hour and a half one way to junior high school by myself, taking two buses each direction every day. My homeroom teacher, Miss Allison, a young white woman with glasses who generally ignored me, would shrug as I walked in ten minutes late, apologizing about a delayed bus. The white kids stared at me in the cafeteria as I gobbled down the horrible school lunch. Who cared. It was all I had to eat.

In this pre-busing era, my siblings and I were unlike most other kids in our neighborhood, traveling miles and miles to largely white, Jewish communities to attend school while our friends walked to the neighborhood school. We grew accustomed to being the only black, or "Negro," in school and were standout students, neat and well-mannered, despite the racist attitudes of many of our teachers, who were happy to knock our 95 test scores down to 85's and 80's over the most trivial mistakes. Being the token Negro was something I was never entirely comfortable with. I was the only black kid in my fifth-grade class at P.S. 138 in the then all-white enclave of Rosedale, Queens, and one afternoon as the teacher dutifully read aloud from our history book's one page on "Negro history," someone in the back of the class whispered, "James is a nigger!" followed by a ripple of tittering and giggling across the room. The teacher shushed him and glared, but the damage had been done. I felt the blood rush to my face and sank low in my chair, seething inside, yet I did nothing. I imagined what my siblings would have done. They would have gone wild. They would have found that punk and bum-rushed him. They never would've allowed anyone to call them a nigger. But I was not them. I was shy and passive and quiet, and only later did the anger come bursting out of me, roaring out of me with such blast-furnace force that I would wonder who that person was and where it all came from.

Music arrived in my life around that time, and books. I would disappear inside whole worlds comprised of *Gulliver's Travels*, *Shane*, and books by Beverly Cleary. I took piano and clarinet lessons in school, often squirreling myself away in some corner with my clarinet to practice, wandering away in Tchaikovsky or John Philip Sousa, trying to improvise like jazz saxophonist James Moody, only to blink back to reality an hour or two later. To further escape from painful reality, I created an imaginary world for myself. I believed my true self was a boy who lived in the mirror. I'd lock myself in the bathroom and spend long hours playing with him. He looked just like me. I'd stare at him. Kiss him. Make faces at him and order him around. Unlike my siblings, he had no opinions. He would listen to me. "If I'm here and you're me, how can *you* be there at the same time?" I'd ask. He'd shrug and smile. I'd shout at him, abuse him verbally. "Give me an answer!" I'd snarl. I would turn to leave, but when I wheeled around he was always there, waiting for me. I had an ache inside, a longing, but I didn't know where it came from or why I had it. The boy in the mirror, he didn't seem to have an ache. He was free. He was never hungry, he had his own bed probably, and his mother wasn't white. I hated him. "Go away!" I'd shout. "Hurry up! Get on out!" but he'd never leave. My siblings would hold their ears to the bathroom door and laugh as I talked to myself. "What a doofus you are," my brother Richie snickered.

Even though my siblings called me "Big Head" because I had a big head and a skinny body, to the outer world I was probably on the "most likely to succeed" list. I was a smart kid. I read a lot. I played music well. I went to church. I had what black folks called "good" hair, because it was curly as opposed to nappy. I was light-skinned or brown-skinned, and girls thought I was cute despite my shyness. Yet I myself had no idea who I was. I loved my mother yet looked nothing like her. Neither did I look like the role models in my life—my step-father, my godparents, other relatives—all of whom were black. And *they* looked nothing like the other heroes I saw, the guys in the movies, white men like Steve McQueen and Paul Newman who beat the bad guys and in the end got the pretty girl—who, incidentally, was always white.

One afternoon I came home from school and cornered Mommy while she was cooking dinner. "Ma, what's a tragic mulatto?" I asked.

Anger flashed across her face like lightning and her nose, which tends to redden and swell in anger, blew up like a balloon. "Where'd you hear that?" she asked.

"I read it in a book."

"For God's sake, you're no tragic mul—What book is this?"

"Just a book I read."

"Don't read that book anymore." She sucked her teeth. "Tragic mulatto. What a stupid thing to call somebody! Somebody called you that?"

"No."

"Don't ever ever use that term."

"Am I black or white?"

"You're a human being," she snapped. "Educate yourself or you'll be a nobody!"

"Will I be a black nobody or just a nobody?"

"If you're a nobody," she said dryly, "it doesn't matter what color you are."

"That doesn't make sense," I said.

She sighed and sat down. "I bet you never heard the joke about the teacher and the beans," she said. I shook my head. "The teacher says to the class, 'Tell us about different kinds of beans.'

"The first little boy says, 'There's pinto beans.'

" 'Correct,' says the teacher.

"Another boy raises his hand. 'There's lima beans.'

" 'Very good,' says the teacher.

"Then a little girl in the back raises her hand and says, 'We're all *human* beans!' "

She laughed. "That's what you are, a *human* bean! And a *fartbuster* to boot!" She got up and went back to cooking, while I wandered away, bewildered.

Perplexed to the point of bursting, I took the question to my elder siblings. Although each had drawn from the same bowl of crazy logic Mommy served up, none seemed to share my own confusion. "Are we black or white?" I asked my brother David one day.

"*I'm* black," said David, sporting his freshly grown Afro the size of Milwaukee. "But *you* may be a Negro. You better check with Billy upstairs."

I approached Billy, but before I could open my mouth, he asked, "Want to see something?"

"Sure," I said.

He led me through our house, past Mommy, who was absorbed in changing diapers, past a pile of upended chairs, books, music stands, and musical instruments that constituted the living room, up the stairs into the boys' bedroom, and over to a closet which was filled, literally, from floor to ceiling, with junk. He stuck his head inside, pointed to the back, and said, "Look at this." When I stuck my head in, he shoved me in from behind and slammed the door, holding it shut. "Hey, man! It's dark in here!" I shouted, banging at the door and trying to keep the fear out of my voice. Suddenly, in the darkness, I felt hands grabbing me and heard a monster roar. My panic zoomed into high-level terror and I frantically pounded on the door with all my might, screaming in a high-pitched, fervent squawk, "BILLLLYYYYYYY!" He released the door and I tore out of the closet, my brother David tumbling out behind me. My two brothers fell to the floor laughing, while I ran around the house crying for Ma, zooming from room to room, my circuits blown.

The question of race was like the power of the moon in my house. It's what made the river flow, the ocean swell, and the tide rise, but it was a silent power, intractable, indomitable, indisputable, and thus completely ignorable. Mommy kept us at a frantic living pace that left no time for the problem. We thrived on thought, books, music, and art, which she fed to us instead of food. At every opportunity she loaded five or six of us onto the subway, paying one fare and pushing the rest of us through the turnstiles while the token-booth clerks frowned and subway riders stared, parading us to every free event New York City offered: festivals, zoos, parades, block parties, libraries, concerts. We walked for hours through the city, long meandering walks that took in whole neighborhoods which we would pass through without buying a thing or speaking to anyone. Twice a year she marched us to the Guggenheim dental clinic in Manhattan for free care, where foreign dental students wearing tunics and armed with drills, picks, and no novocaine, manned a row of dental chairs and reduced each of us to a screaming mass of tears while the others waited in line, watching, horrified. They pulled teeth like maniacs, barking at us in whatever their native tongues were while they yanked our heads back and forth like rag dolls'. They once pulled my brother Billy's tooth and then sent him out to Ma in the waiting room, whereupon she looked into the mouth full of gauze and blood and discovered they had yanked the wrong tooth. She marched back in and went wild. In summer she was the Pied Piper, leading the whole pack of us to public swimming pools, stripping down to her one-piece bathing suit and plunging into the water like a walrus, the rest of us following her like seals, splashing and gurgling in terror behind her as Mommy flailed along, seemingly barely able to swim herself until one of us coughed and sputtered, at which time she whipped through the water and grabbed the offending child, pulling him out and slapping him on the back, laughing. We did not consider ourselves poor or deprived, or depressed, for the rules of the outside world seemed meaningless to us as children. But as we grew up and fanned out into the world as teenagers and college students, we brought the outside world home with us, and the world that Mommy had so painstakingly created began to fall apart.

The sixties roared through my house like a tidal wave. My sister Helen's decision to drop out of school and run off at age fifteen, though she returned home five years later with a nursing degree and a baby girl, was the first sign of impending doom. Now the others began to act out, and the sense of justice and desire for equal rights that Mommy and my father had imparted to us began to backfire. Kind, gentle, Sunday school children who had been taught to say proudly, "I am a Negro," and recite the deeds of Jackie Robinson and Paul Robeson now turned to Malcolm X and H. Rap Brown and Martin Luther King for inspiration. Mommy was the wrong color for black pride and black power, which nearly rent my house in two.

One by one, my elder siblings broke with her rules, coming home bearing fruits of their own confusion, which we jokingly called their "revolution." An elder brother disappeared to Europe. Another sister had an affair at college and came home with a love child, fairly big news in 1967. My brother Richie got married at eighteen over Mommy's objections, divorced, then entered college, and was home on summer break when he got stopped by two cops while walking down the street with a friend. A group of boys who were walking about ten yards in front of Richie and his friend had ditched what appeared to be a bag of heroin as the cop car approached. The cops grouped the boys together, lined them up against a fence, and demanded to know which of them had jettisoned the bag, which later turned out to be filled with quinine, not heroin. All denied it, so the cops searched them all and found ninety dollars of Richie's college-bank-loan money in his pocket. When the policeman asked him where he got the money from, Richie told him it was his college money and he'd forgotten he'd had it. If you knew Richie, you'd nod and say, "Uh-huh," because it was perfectly in character for him to forget he was carrying around ninety precious dollars, which was a huge sum in those days. We used to call him "the Mad Scientist" when he was little. His science experiments would nearly blow up the house because whatever he created, he'd leave it bubbling and boiling while he went to search for food, forgetting it completely. He could remember the toughest calculus formulas and had nearly perfect pitch as a musician, but he literally could not remember to put his pants on. He would play John Coltrane–type solos on his sax for hours and be dressed in a winter jacket and gym shorts the whole time. He was that kind of kid, absentminded, and very smart, and later in life he became a chemist. But to the cops, he was just another black perpetrator with a story, and he was arrested and jailed.

Mommy paced the house all night when she got the news. She showed up early at Richie's arraignment the next day and took a seat right behind the defense table. When they brought him out in hand-cuffs and she saw him cuffed and dirty after being in the holding pen all night, she could not contain her grief and began muttering like a crazy woman, wringing her hands. Through her reverie of mumbo jumbo she heard the court-appointed lawyer lean over to Richie and offer two words of legal advice: "Plead guilty." She jumped up and screamed, "Wait!" She charged past the court officers, shouting to the judge that it was a mistake, that none of her kids had ever been in trouble with the law before, that her son was a college student, and so forth. The white judge, who had noticed Mommy sitting in the largely black courtroom, released Richie to her custody and the charges were later dropped.

But that experience made Mommy bear down on the younger ones like me even more. She was, in retrospect, quite brilliant when it came to manipulating us. She depended heavily on the "king/queen system" which she established in our house long before I was born: the eldest sibling was the king or queen and you could not defy him or her, because you were a slave. When the eldest left for college, the next ascended to the throne. The king/queen system gave us a sense of order, rank, and self. It gave the older ones the sense that they were in charge, when in actuality it was Mommy who ruled the world. It also harked back to her own traditional Orthodox upbringing where the home was run by one dominating figure with strict rules and regula-tions. Despite the orchestrated chaos of our home, we always ate meals at a certain time, always did homework at a certain time, and always went to bed at a certain time. Mommy also aligned herself with any relative or friend who had any interest in any of her children and would send us off to stay with whatever relative promised to straighten us out, and many did. The extended black family was Mommy's hole card, and she played it as often as the times demanded because her family was not available to her. As I grew older, it occurred to me at some point that we had some relatives we had never seen. "How come we don't have any aunts and uncles on your side?" I asked her one day.

"I had a brother who died and my sister . . . I don't know where she is," she said.

"Why not?"

"We got separated."

"How's that?"

"I'm removed from my family."

"Removed?"

"Removed. Dead."

"Who's dead?'

"I'm dead. They're dead too by now probably. What's the difference? They didn't want me to marry on the black side."

"But if you're black already, how can they be mad at you?"

Boom. I had her. But she ignored it. "Don't ask me any more questions."

My stepfather, a potential source of information about her background, was not helpful. "Oh, your mama, you mind her," he grunted when I asked him. He loved her. He seemed to have no problem with her being white, which I found odd, since she was clearly so different from him. Whereas he was largely easygoing and open-minded about most worldly matters, she was suspicious, strict, and inaccessible. Whenever she stepped out of the house with us, she went into a sort of mental zone where her attention span went no farther than the five kids trailing her and the tightly balled fist in which she held her small bit of money, which she always counted to the last penny. She had absolutely no interest in a world that seemed incredibly agitated by our presence. The stares and remarks, the glances and cackles that we heard as we walked about the world went right over her head, but not over mine. By age ten, I was coming into my own feelings about myself and my own impending manhood, and going out with Mommy, which had been a privilege and an honor at age five, had become a dreaded event. I had reached a point where I was ashamed of her and didn't want the world to see my white mother. When I went out with my friends, I'd avoid telling her where we were playing because I didn't want her coming to the park to fetch me. I grew secretive, cautious, passive, angry, and fearful, always afraid that the baddest cat on the block would call her a "honky," in which case I'd have to respond and get my ass kicked. "Come and let's walk to the store," she said one afternoon.

"I can go by myself," I said. The intent was to hide my white mom and go it alone.

"Okay," she said. She didn't seem bothered by my newfound independence. Relieved, I set off to a neighborhood grocery store. The store owner was a gruff white man who, like many of the whites in St. Albans, was on his way out as we blacks began to move in. He did not seem to like black children and he certainly took no particular liking to or interest in me. When I got home, Mommy placed the quart of milk he sold me on the table, opened it up, and the smell of sour milk filled the room. She closed the carton and handed it to me. "Take it back and get my money back."

"Do I have to?"

"Take it back." It was an order. I was a Little Kid in my house, not a Big Kid who could voice opinions and sway the master. I had to take orders.

I dragged myself back to the store, dreading the showdown I knew was coming. The owner glared at me when I walked in. "I have to return this," I said.

"Not here," he said. "The milk is opened. I'm not taking it back."

I returned home. Ten minutes later Mommy marched into the store, doing her "madwalk," the bowlegged strut that meant thunder and lightning was coming—body pitched forward, jaw jutted out, hands balled into tight fists, nose red, stomping like Cab Calloway with the Billy Eckstein band blowing full blast behind him. I followed her sheepishly, my plan to go it alone and hide my white mother now completely awash, backfired in the worst way.

She angrily placed the milk on the counter. The merchant looked at her, then at me. Then back at her. Then at me again. The surprise written on his face changed to anger and disgust, and it took me completely by surprise. I thought the man would see Ma, think they had something in common, then give her the dough and we'd be off. "That milk is sold," he said.

"Smell it," Ma said. "It's spoiled."

"I don't smell milk. I sell milk."

Right away they were at each other, I mean really going at it. A crowd of black kids gathered, watching my white mother arguing with this white man. I wanted to sink into the floor and disappear. "It's okay, Ma . . ." I said. She ignored me. In matters of money, of which she had so little, I knew it was useless. She was going full blast— ". . . fool . . . think you are . . . idiot!"—her words flying together like gibberish, while the neighborhood kids howled, woofing like dogs and enjoying the show.

After a while it was clear the man was not going to return her money, so she grabbed my hand and was heading toward the door, when he made another remark, something that I missed, something he murmured beneath his breath so softly that I couldn't hear, but it made the crowd murmur "Ooohhhh." Ma stiffened. Still holding the milk in her right hand, she turned around and flung it at him like a football. He ducked and the milk missed him, smashing into the cigarette cabinet behind him and sending milk and cigarettes splattering everywhere.

I could not understand such anger. I could not understand why she didn't just give up the milk. Why cause a fuss? I thought. My own embarrassment overrode all other feelings. As I walked home, holding Mommy's hand while she fumed, I thought it would be easier if we were just one color, black or white. I didn't want to be white. My siblings had already instilled the notion of black pride in me. I would have preferred that Mommy were black. Now, as a grown man, I feel privileged to have come from two worlds. My view of the world is not merely that of a black man but that of a black man with something of a Jewish soul. I don't consider myself Jewish, but when I look at Holocaust photographs of Jewish women whose children have been wrenched from them by Nazi soldiers, the women look like my own mother and I think to myself, *There but for the grace of God goes my own mother—and by extension, myself.* When I see two little Jewish old ladies giggling over coffee at a Manhattan diner, it makes me smile, because I hear my own mother's laughter beneath theirs. Conversely, when I hear black "leaders" talking about "Jewish slave owners" I feel angry and disgusted, knowing that they're inflaming people with lies and twisted history, as if all seven of the Jewish slave owners in the antebellum South, or however few there were, are responsible for the problems of African-Americans now. Those leaders are no better than their Jewish counterparts who spin statistics in marvelous ways to make African-Americans look like savages, criminals, drags on society, and "animals" (a word quite popular when used to describe blacks these days). I don't belong to any of those groups. I belong to the world of one God, one people. But as a kid, I preferred the black side, and often wished that Mommy had sent me to black schools like my friends. Instead I was stuck at that white school, P.S. 138, with white classmates who were convinced I could dance like James Brown. They constantly badgered me to do the "James Brown" for them, a squiggling of the feet made famous by the "Godfather of Soul" himself, who back in the sixties was bigger than life. I tried to explain to them that I couldn't dance. I have always been one of the worst dancers that God has ever put upon this earth. My sisters would spend hours at home trying out new dances to Archie Bell and the Drells, Martha Reeves, King Curtis, Curtis Mayfield, Aretha Franklin, and the Spinners. "Come on and dance!" they'd shout, boogying across the room. Even Ma would join in, sashaying across the floor, but when I joined in I looked so odd and stupid they fell to the floor laughing. "Give it up," they said. "You can't dance."

The white kids in school did not believe me, and after weeks of encouragement I found myself standing in front of the classroom on talent day, wearing my brother's good shoes and hitching up my pants, soul singer–style like one of the Temptations, as someone dropped the needle on a James Brown record. I slid around the way I'd seen him do, shouting "Owww—shabba-na!" They were delighted. Even the teacher was amused. They really believed I could dance! I had them fooled. They screamed for more and I obliged, squiggling my feet and slip-sliding across the wooden floor, jumping into the air and landing in a near split by the blackboard, shouting "Eeeee-yowwww!" They went wild, but even as I sat down with their applause ringing in my ears, with laughter on my face, happy to feel accepted, to be part of them, knowing I had pleased them, I saw the derision on their faces, the clever smiles, laughing at the oddity of it, and I felt the same ache I felt when I gazed at the boy in the mirror. I remembered him, and how free he was, and I hated him even more.

11.

Boys

If there was one thing Tateh didn't like more than gentiles, it was black folks. And if there was one thing he didn't like more than black folks in general, it was black men in particular. So it stands to reason that the first thing I fell in love with in life was a black man. I didn't do it on purpose. I was a rebellious little girl in my own quiet way, but I wasn't so rebellious that I wanted to risk my own life or anybody else's life. They would kill a black man for looking at a white woman in the South in those days. They'd hang him. And the girl, they'd run her out of town. Who wants trouble like that? But as I became a teenager, I wanted the same things any teenage girl wants. I wanted love, nice clothes, a date. I never had that. My life was the store. My life hadn't changed since elementary school. The only break I got was when Mameh would send me to her relatives in New York during summers, but in fact, my responsibility for the store grew after my brother Sam ran off. My daily routine never changed: Open the store at seven, school till three, come straight home and work till ten, then flop to sleep. Work all through the weekend except the Sabbath, then back to school on Monday. My only freedom was to swipe pennies from the store drawer and walk downtown with Dee-Dee to buy romance magazines like True Love and True Romance. They used to tear the front cover off the back issues of the romance magazines and sell them by the bundle for ten cents. We'd read them on the Sabbath by candlelight. You couldn't light a stove, or play, or tear paper, or ride in a car on the Sabbath, but you could read.

It wasn't like I had a great family life to turn to. We went to synagogue together on Saturday morning and Jewish holidays, but Tateh didn't love Mameh. His idea of a family outing was to take me and my sister to a chicken farm in Portsmouth, Virginia, where he'd slaughter chickens according to kosher law so he could sell them to Jewish customers. He would sit on a low box or stool, pick up the chicken, hold it by its neck faceup, and slit it across the neck. Then he'd toss it away and grab another one while the headless chicken would fluff and flap around, give a few heavy shakes, and die.

I was never asked out for a date by anyone in school. I loved to dance and had long legs, and I once auditioned for a dance musical at school and made it, but some of the girls made such a fuss over having to dance next to a Jew that I dropped out of it. During gym class when we'd pick tennis partners, the girls would pick and pick until I'd be standing alone. If Frances wasn't around, I wouldn't get picked. I'd like to say I didn't care about my classmates, and what they thought of me. But when I was a teenager I wanted to be like them—American and WASP and going around in style, going dancing, but my parents wouldn't have that. Dancing? Forget it. New clothes? No way. Tateh was the one who decided what clothes we wore, and he'd buy the cheapest things he could find. He was used to us getting hand-me-downs from the congregations and that was fine with him. He'd buy a brand new V-8 car every year but he couldn't see the logic in buying new clothes when you got cheap hand-me-downs for free. I once wanted these white moccasin-type shoes that were the fashion in those days, and I bothered Tateh to buy them for me so much he got sick of me and relented. We went downtown and the clerk showed us a pair two sizes too big. I put them on and said, "They're perfect."

Tateh looked at me like I was crazy. "They're too big," he said.

"This is how they're supposed to fit," I said. I was afraid he would change his mind. And the clerk, he wanted to sell those things and make his money, so he babbled out, "Oh, they're perfect, Reverend Shilsky, they're perfect."

Tateh grumbled about it, but he paid for them.

The moccasins were so big my feet squeaked and squished in them, like they'd been plunged in a bucket of water. I went squishing down the hallway in school and the kids laughed at them, so I took them off.

None of the boys in school would even bother with me. So after a while I had me my own friend, and he didn't care that I wore secondhand clothes or was Jewish. He never judged me. That's the first thing I liked about him, in fact that's what I liked about black folks all my life: They never judged me. My black friends never asked me how much money I made, or what school my children went to, or anything like that. They just said, "Come as you are." Blacks have always been peaceful and trusting. I don't care what they show on TV, these stupid boys with guns and these murderers they show on the news. Those aren't the majority. Most blacks are peaceful and trusting. That's why they're made a fool of so easily.

My boyfriend's name was Peter, and he lived in one of the houses on the road behind the store. He was a tall, handsome young man, dark-skinned with beautiful teeth and a beautiful smile. He'd come into the store and buy Coca-Colas, crackers, gum, or other small items. I didn't notice him at first because I was always busy when he came in the store. There was plenty of work to do, not just behind the counter but elsewhere; like the wholesalers used to sell margarine without the yellow in it, so I'd have to go in the back and add the yellow dye to it, stir it around in a big barrel, or go into the ice freezer and pull out big blocks of meat and ice to chop up and lay out, just any number of things. But he'd come and find me in the store alone somehow and he'd linger, chatting or teasing me and trying to get me to smile in some way. He had a sense of humor that made me laugh all the time, and I began to look forward to his coming by. He'd always make sure Tateh and Mameh weren't around, which was difficult because Tateh kept a close eye on his daughters, but Peter would find his moments. One day he saw me outside pumping kerosene out of the tank and he came around and asked me to go for a walk and I said yes. He was a bold guy because from that moment on he was risking his life. God knows what I was thinking about. The only thing I told him was, "If my father sees us, we're in trouble." Tateh with his loaded pistol would've shot him certainly, and probably me, too, but it didn't matter to me. I was naive and young and before you know it I fell in love with him.

I loved that boy to death and he loved me. At least, I thought he did. Who cared that he was black? He was the first man other than my grandfather who ever showed me any kindness in my life, and he did it at the risk of his own because they would've strung him up faster than you can blink if they'd have found out. Not just the Ku Klux Klan but the regular white folks in town would've killed him. Half of them were probably the Klan anyway, so it was all the same. You know death was always around Suffolk, always around. It was always so hot, and everyone was so polite, and everything was all surface but underneath it was like a bomb waiting to go off. I always felt that way about the South, that beneath the smiles and southern hospitality and politeness were a lot of guns and liquor and secrets. A lot of those secrets ended up floating down the Nansemond River just down the road from us. Folks would go down to the wharf and throw out nets for crabs and turtles and haul in human bodies. I remember one of our customers, Mrs. Mayfield, they found her son out there, he wasn't more than seventeen or so. He'd been killed and tied to a wagon wheel and tossed into the water until he drowned or the crabs ate him. You know a crab will eat anything. You have never seen me eat a crab to this day and you never will.

Well, Peter and I were having our regular little secret rendezvous, carefully arranged. We'd meet in the yard or the passage behind the store, or he'd write a note and slip it to me secretly. If the store was closed he'd slide the note under the front door. On the Sabbath, Friday nights, it was a thrill for me to pretend I was going downstairs to the kitchen and then creep into the store to pick up the torrid love notes he slipped under the door. He would pledge his love for me no matter what and write out the plan for our secret meeting. At the appointed time he'd come by and pick me up in a car and I'd get into the back seat and lie flat so I wouldn't be seen. He had friends that lived out in the country in isolated areas, and that's where we would be together.

You know, my whole life changed after I fell in love. It was like the sun started shining on me for the first time, and for the first time in my life I began to smile. I was loved, I was loved, and I didn't care what anyone thought. I wasn't worried about getting caught, but I did notice that Peter's friends were terrified of me; they stayed clear anytime I came near them. They'd walk away from me if they saw me walking down the road coming toward them, and if they came into the store, they wouldn't even look at me. That started to worry me a little but I didn't worry much. Then after a while, my period was late. By a week.

Then another two weeks.

Then it never came.

Well, the whole thing just started to unravel on me then. I was pregnant and couldn't tell a soul. The white folks would have killed him and my father would have killed him. I had maybe just turned fifteen then. There wasn't a person I could tell. I'd wake up in the middle of the night, just sit straight up in bed in a sweat, and go outside to the back balcony to hide my tears from my sister. I did consider telling Frances, but that was too much to ask. This was 1936. I mean, what I did was way, way out as far as white folks were concerned. It was trouble. I couldn't bring Frances into that. There was no one to tell. I'd just sit there on the balcony at night while everyone slept and cry and watch the moon. I never thought to kill myself, never that. But I'd cry for a while and after I was finished crying I'd look out over the black section of town for my boyfriend. Can you believe that? I was in it thick, up to my neck, and I'm still looking for my boyfriend. I thought he had all the answers.

If there was moonlight, you could see out there, down the back roads behind our store where the black folks lived, and from the balcony I'd look for him. I knew how he walked and moved and dressed and everything. I could recognize him at a distance from his walk; I'd look to see if he was safe at home, because I'd always heard the Klan *comes at night to get you, and after they found that Mayfield boy floating in the wharf tied to that wagon wheel I worried about him. I'd sit up half the night expecting the Klan to come riding past the store in those tin lizzie Model A cars and what would I do if they did? I had no idea. The law wasn't for the black man in Virginia in those days, it was against him.*

You know, the thing was, I was supposed to be white and "number one," too. That was a big thing in the South. You're white, and even if you're a Jew, since you're white you're better than a so-called colored. Well, I didn't feel number one with nobody but him, and I didn't give a hoot that he was black. He was kind! And good! I knew that! And I wanted to tell folks that, I wanted to shout out, "Hey y'all, it really doesn't matter!" I actually believed folks would accept that, that they'd see what a good person he was and maybe accept us, and I went through a few days of thinking this, after which I told him one night, "Let's run off to the country and get married," and he said, "No way. I don't know where that's been done before, white and black marrying in Virginia. They will surely hang me."

I grew really frightened then. Because he'd never talked that way before, and I could see he was afraid. He said, "If white folks find out you're pregnant by me, I will surely hang."

The truth hit me hard then, when I realized he didn't have any solutions, and I began to panic. What a fool I was to believe we could get away with it! I'd sit on the balcony chastising myself a million times for what I'd done and waiting for the Klan to come kill him and for my father to kill both of us, but the days passed and nothing happened. I said to myself, "We are lucky no white folks know about us." I was sure none knew. Some black folks knew, some of Peter's friends, but none of the white folks knew.

None except for one.

There was one white person who did know.

Peter and I used to meet in an alley behind the store, and one night we were back there arguing about what to do and I dropped my bracelet on the ground. It was a cheap little dime store bracelet but I bought it with my own money and I liked it. It was pitch-black there and we couldn't find it without a match or a light, so we left it. When I went out there to find it the next day, it was gone.

Mameh came up to me in the store a couple of days later while I was standing behind the counter and placed the bracelet on the counter. Real quiet. Just placed it on the counter and limped back to her little chair by the door where she always sat in her apron, sorting and stacking vegetables.

"Why don't you go to New York this summer to see your grandmother?" she said.

12.

Daddy

At some point in my consciousness, it occured to me that I had a father. It happened around the time my younger brother Hunter was born. I was five years ahead of Hunter, and while the arrival of a new baby in the house didn't seem to shake anyone—Hunter was the eleventh child—it was the first time that an elderly, slow-moving man in a brown hat, vest sweater, suspenders, and wool pants seemed to float into my consciousness. He picked up Hunter and held him in the air with such delight it made me happy to watch him. His name was Hunter Jordan, Sr., and he raised me as his own son.

As a small boy, I was never quite aware of the concept of "father." My real father, Andrew McBride, died before I was born. I was lorded over by Mommy, my older siblings, friends of Ma's, and relatives on my father's and stepfather's sides whom, years later, I would recognize as guiding forces in my life. Out of this haze of relatives and authority figures loomed a dominating presence that would come and go. My stepfather worked as a furnace fireman for the New York City Housing Authority, fixing and maintaining the huge boilers that heated the Red Hook Housing Projects where we lived then. He and Mommy met a few months after my biological father died; Ma was selling church dinners in the plaza in front of our building at 811 Hicks Street when my stepfather came by and bought a rib dinner. The next week he came back and bought another, then another and another. He must have been getting sick eating all those ribs. Finally one afternoon he came by where she was selling the church dinners and asked Ma, "Do you go to the movies?"

"Yeah," she said. "But I got eight kids and they go to the movies too."

"You got enough for a baseball team," he said.

He married her and made the baseball team his own, adding four more kids to make it an even twelve. He made no separation between the McBride and Jordan children, and my siblings and I never thought of or referred to each other as half brothers and sisters; for the powerless Little Kids, myself included, he was "Daddy." For the midlevel executives, he was sometimes "Daddy," sometimes "Mr. Hunter." To the powerful elder statesmen who remembered their biological father well, he was always "Mr. Hunter." The older ones liked to make fun of "Mr. Hunter," the slow way he moved, the southern accent. "Hrrrfffff! Hrrrrffffff!" they'd say when he was out of earshot. But they loved and appreciated him.

When I was about six or seven, he came to our apartment in the projects, piled us into his car, and drove us out to St. Albans, Queens, parking in front of a large, pink stucco, four-bedroom house and disappearing inside while we played on the big front lawn, tearing out the grass and rolling around in the leaves. It was fall, and leaves were everywhere. After a while he came outside and sat on the stoop and watched us play. We tore the grass to shreds, crushed the neatly manicured bushes, stomped the flowers, and cracked one of the house's windows with a rock. After ravaging the lawn for about an hour, one of us had the presence of mind to ask him, "Whose house is this?" He laughed. I never saw him laugh so hard. He had just spent his life's savings to buy the place.

He was a gruff man with a good sense of humor, quiet, and stuck in his ways. He liked neatness, which meant our St. Albans house was out of bounds for him. However much he loved us, he couldn't live with the madness in our Queens home, preferring to keep his old digs at 478 Carlton Avenue in Fort Greene, Brooklyn. He came home only on weekends, striding into the living room with bags of groceries, Entenmann's cakes, a pocketful of dough, and a real live automobile parked outside, in which he often piled in as many of us as would fit to take us back to his brownstone for the weekend. We loved staying in his house in Brooklyn. It was old and dark and filled with antique furniture, cookies, and Nat King Cole records.

His father was a black man, a railroad brakeman, and his mother a Native American, so he had a lot of Indian in his face: brown skin, slanted brown eyes, high cheekbones, and a weather-beaten outdoor look about him, a very handsome dude. He was educated in a one-room schoolhouse and raised on a farm in Henrico County, near Richmond, Virginia, and his family, the Jordans, were easygoing folks. Beneath their cool exterior, however, was a rugged breed of black man you did not want to cross—tough, grizzled men whose strong brown hands gripped hammers tightly and whose eyes met you dead on.

Those hands could fix anything that cranked, moved, pumped heat, moved water, or had valves, vacuums, or wires.

He fled Virginia around 1927 or so, with Jim Crow hot on his tail, so to speak. A white sheriff had locked him up for peeking under the tent of a traveling circus without paying, and when the sheriff went to lunch and inadvertently left the cell door open, Daddy eased out of the jailhouse and caught the first thing smokin'; he never returned to Virginia for good until he died. He met up with his brother Walter in Chicago, where he was fleeced and pickpocketed from the time he hit town till the time he left. He worked in slaughterhouses there, moved up to Detroit, where he shined shoes with his brother in a barbershop near the Ford plant—he shined one of Henry Ford's shoes while Walter shined the other—and on to Brooklyn, New York, in the Roaring Twenties, where the brothers made a living selling illegal booze for a while. He was out of his apartment one day when one of his liquor-making stills broke and spilled so much liquor onto the floor that it leaked downstairs into the apartment below; the guy living downstairs held his glass under his light fixture and got dead drunk, wandering into the street while my stepfather tried to reel him in, but the cat was out of the bag and not long after that he was raided. He jumped out his back window holding two five-gallon jugs of hooch, right into the arms of waiting federal agents. He did time for that, something neither he nor Mommy ever told us about, though I always wondered how a guy who seemed so unsophisticated could be so clever at checkers. I never could beat him.

Altogether there were four brothers—he, Henry, Walter, and Garland—and they epitomized old-time cool: suave, handsome black men who worked hard, drank hard, dressed well, liked fine women and new money. Daddy's favorite was Walter, the most fun-loving and gregarious of his brothers. He'd often take us to Walter's house in Fort

Greene just blocks from his house, where my siblings and I would play with our cousin Little Mommy while Uncle Walter, Daddy, and their other brothers partied, drinking and listening to Nat King Cole, Gene Krupa, and Charlie Parker records. Mommy would never drink at these occasions. She did not like us to socialize too much with the partying side of Daddy's family. She never drank or smoked. In fact, drinking was number one on her don't list, and if my stepfather drank too much, she'd scream at him on the way home. He'd drive twenty miles an hour all the way to Queens from Brooklyn, nosing his big sedan through traffic till he found a city bus, which he would get behind and follow all the way home. "You can never get a speeding ticket if you follow one of them," he declared. Car after car of angry motorists would fly by us, yelling, "GET OFF THE DAMN ROAD!" He'd ignore them. We'd be in the back seat, shrinking low, laughing, hoping none of our friends would happen to see us.

Every summer he would take a bunch of us down south to Richmond to his cousin Clemy's house, where we ate watermelon from Clemy's yard, rode her pony, and watched our other "down south" relatives do wild tricks, like taking their teeth out. We had a cousin who would sit on the couch, drink a beer, and take her teeth out, making them go *chomp! chomp!* and causing us to run from the room. Uncle Henry was a real character. He was a mechanic and a decorated World War II vet who had a gold tooth in his mouth that flashed and sparkled when he smiled, which was often. His stomach had been ruined after he was stabbed in a knife fight, though I couldn't imagine him angry. We loved him. When he laughed, he sounded like a car trying to start, "Heeerrrrrrr! Heerrrrrrrr!" We used to make fun of his laugh, which amused him greatly, touching off another round of "Heeerrrrrr! Heerrrrrrr!" from him, prompting further outraged giggles from us.

There were so many of us, we'd travel south in two cars, some of us riding with Daddy and Mommy in Daddy's car, some with Walter and Henry in a second car. One night as we began one of our migrations back to New York from Richmond, Uncle Henry got drunk and was driving at a hundred miles an hour in his Oldsmobile with me, my sister Judy, and my Uncle Walter inside. "This baby's a powerhouse!" he roared, stomping the accelerator and flying up Interstate 95 as I watched Daddy's headlights through the back windshield grow dimmer and dimmer, then disappear altogether. As he barreled up the road laughing, Uncle Walter screamed at him, "Henry, slow down, dammit!" Uncle Henry ignored him for a few more harrowing minutes, finally pulling over at a rest stop. Minutes later Daddy's car, full of Mommy and the rest of the kids, screeched up behind us. Daddy jumped out of his car so fast his hat flew off.

"Goddammit, Henry!" Walter had to restrain Daddy, and Henry, the boldest of the brothers, backed off and apologized. Daddy was the most respected of the brothers, and anger was a rarity with him. He had a peaceful, strong manner that did not provoke anger or invite fights. We drove back to New York packed in Daddy's car, while Henry slept peacefully in the back of his own car with Walter driving. Walter offered to take a couple of us with him but Daddy refused. "I had enough of y'all," he said. Walter shrugged.

I thought my stepfather was odd. The fact that he and Mommy seemed to love one another did not help me think differently. He was nothing like my friends' parents, who were younger, drove new cars, followed the Mets, talked about civil rights, and foot-raced with us. He had no idea of what the sixties meant, nor did they seem to interest him. His only interests were my grades and church. He came to my church confirmation alone because Mommy could not, dressed to the nines, shirt buttoned to the top, hat creased just so, and sat in the back by himself, paying no attention to the other, younger fathers dressed in bell-bottoms and hip sixties wear. He greeted my Sunday school teacher respectfully, hat in hand, and she smiled at him, impressed by his handsomeness and cool manner. But when she tried to engage him in conversation he seemed uninterested, taking my hand and backing away, his gestures saying, "Thanks, but no thanks." He went to my eldest brother Dennis's college graduation dressed in his old-timey clothes and walked around the all-black campus of Lincoln University in Pennsylvania beaming, full of so much pride, his family and white wife in tow, as black students and their parents did double takes. I used to look at him and wonder, *What is his problem? Doesn't he know how goofy he looks?* but it never seemed to bother him in the least. Race was something he never talked about. To him it was a detail that you stepped over, like a crack in the sidewalk. He was a person who never seemed to worry. "Everything's gonna be allllllll riiiiight," he'd say. That was his motto.

Then in 1969 he got a letter from the city of New York telling him to move out of his house in Brooklyn. They were planning to build a low-income-housing high rise there. He was stunned. He had renovated that old brownstone from a shell. It was his refuge, his joy, his hobby. They gave him $13,000 and he was gone. Twenty years later when I moved back to Fort Greene—now immortalized by Spike Lee's movies, with gentrification pushing poor blacks out and brownstones selling for $350,000—I'd walk by 478 Carlton Avenue and look at the empty lot there. Nothing. A total waste.

When they tore down his house, it was like they ripped out half his arteries. He came to Queens and lived with us, converting a piece of the basement into his old-time headquarters; he squeezed in his antique furniture, his windup record player, and a small refrigerator in which he stored his jars of pig feet and cans of Rheingold beer, but his heart was back in Brooklyn. He'd retired by then—he was seventy-two—but he did odd jobs and worked on heating systems with his brother Walter. One night about three years after he moved in with us, he was staggering around the kitchen, cursing and saying his head hurt, and before I knew it, an ambulance pulled up and they were loading him in. "What's wrong with him?" I asked Ma. She said nothing, her eyes red-rimmed, denoting deep alarm, as she climbed into the ambulance with his sweater grasped tightly in her fist.

He'd had a stroke. I was fourteen and didn't know what a stroke was. I thought it was something you got from the sun. For me, the two weeks or so he was in the hospital meant I could hang out with my friends as long and as late as I wanted to, and I avoided going to see him until Mommy forced me to. I went with my sister Kathy, and when we walked into his hospital room, it was a brutal shock. He was laid out in hospital white. His face was slightly twisted. He could not talk. He could not move his right arm or right side. His hand, a strong, brown, veined hand that I'd seen gripping wrenches and tools and pipe fittings hundreds of times, was nearly limp, covered with IV gauze and connected to an IV. Mommy sat by him in silence, her face ashen. Kathy, who was always his favorite, walked into the room, saw him, and backed away from him, horrified. She could not look at him. She sat on a chair near the window and stared outside, crying softly. He raised his hand to comfort her and made some sort of horrid, gurgling speech noise to get her attention. She finally came over to him and laid her head on his chest and wept uncontrollably. I walked out of the room, wiping my tears, staggering toward the elevator, covering my eyes so no one could see, as nurses and hospital aides backed out of my way.

He came home from the hospital about a week later and seemed to get better. His speech, though slurred, returned. He sat in his base-ment headquarters, recuperating, while we crept around the house and Mommy walked about silently, eyes still red-rimmed, on edge. One day he summoned me downstairs and asked me to help him dress. "I want to take a drive," he said. I was the oldest kid living at home by then, my other siblings being away at school. He put on his sweater, wool pants, hat, and blue peacoat. Though ill and thin, he still looked sharp. Slowly, he mounted the stairs and stepped outside. It was May and brisk, almost cold outside. We went into the garage and stepped into his gold-colored Pontiac. "I want to drive home one more time," he said. He was talking about Richmond, Virginia, where he grew up. But he was too weak to drive, so he sat there behind the wheel of the car, staring at the garage wall, and he began to talk.

He said he had a little money saved up for Mommy and a little land in Virginia, but it was not enough. He said that since I was the oldest living at home, I had to watch out for Mommy and my little brothers and sisters because "y'all are special," he said. "And just so special to me." It was the only time I ever heard him refer to race in any way, however vaguely, but it didn't matter, because right then and there I knew he was going to die and I had to blink back my tears. I wanted to tell him that I loved him, that I hoped with all my heart that he would get better, but I could not formulate the words in my mouth. We had never spoken that way to one another. We joked and talked, but his chief concern had always been my "schoolin'" and "church raising" as he called it. He was not a man for dialogue. That was Mommy's job.

Two days later he suffered a relapse. An ambulance came and got him. About four in the morning the phone rang. My sister Kathy and I lay upstairs and listened, and through what seemed to be a fog, I heard my older brother Richie telling Mommy, "It's all right, Ma. It's all right."

"It's not all right! It's not all right!" Ma cried, and she wailed and wailed, the sound of her cries circling the house like a spirit and settling on all the corridors and beds where we lay, weeping in silence.

13.

New York

My mother knew I was pregnant and in trouble. Looking back, she knew. All she did was sit by the door of the store all day and fix up the vegetables and watch out for her two daughters. Dee-Dee and I were two young girls and there were men everywhere and she knew. She never said a word about it either. Mameh wasn't a pushy woman. She was quiet and watchful. She had that polio, you know, and used to drape a towel over her twisted left hand sometimes to hide it when she walked around. She was nearly blind in one eye and had occasional fainting spells, but she wasn't weak-minded. She saw I was unhappy down there and had started sending me up to New York practically every summer by Greyhound to stay with her family. The fare was only nineteen dollars one way.

   Mameh had five sisters and one brother in New York, plus her mother, and they all were living high. My Aunt Laura and her husband, Paul Schiffman, they owned apartment buildings in the Bronx and Harlem. My Uncle Hal owned a kosher delicatessen in Brooklyn. Aunt Bernadette married a furrier, and Aunt Mary opened up a leather factory. Now they were a funny family. They kept their feelings secret, bottled up inside them till they swelled and burst out like a water balloon you squeeze. I had two aunts, Bernadette and Rhonda, who hadn't spoken to each other in fifteen years. I don't know why. It was a big secret and you weren't supposed to ask. I never did.

My aunts never wanted to be bothered with me too much. I was the daughter of their poor crippled sister. I was the poor cousin from the South. They called us, Mameh's family, "greenhorns" in Yiddish, because we were the last to get to America and weren't Americanized, but still I liked to visit them because New York was an eyepopper for me. Plus everyone seemed too busy to care about what race or religion you were. I loved it.

I had never seen so many people rushing about. I would say to myself, "Where the heck they gotta be, rushing like that?" But I wanted to rush like them, and got with the program as soon as I could. Sometimes I'd just go out and walk with them so I could rush with the crowd. I had nowhere to go. Just going crazy, rushing with the rest!

I would stay with my grandmother, or Aunt Mary or Aunt Laura when I visited. Aunt Laura was the oldest and richest of my mother's sisters, a meticulous woman and a fabulous dresser who wore white gloves and beautifully colored dresses. She lived in a huge apartment on West End Avenue in Manhattan with shiny hardwood floors, beautiful mahogany furniture, and a live-in German maid who cooked and kept house, though no one could clean Aunt Laura's house better than Aunt Laura herself. She had no aversion to housework. She'd get on her hands and knees and scrub her kitchen floor till it shone. The meals would be served in courses by the maid while you sat there, and you had to ask to be excused from the table. Her family spent summers at Rockaway Beach or Edgemere, where they had a small cottage about eight blocks from the water. Anybody who was anybody was supposed to have a cottage by the beach.

Aunt Mary lived on the Grand Concourse in the Bronx and ran a factory that made leather trimmings for fur coats, jackets, muffs, hats, and other wearables (Hercules Skivving or Trimming Company). I worked in her factory, running a machine that cut belts. Plus I did other odds and ends for Aunt Mary, whatever she ordered me to do. She was as mean to me as the day was long—"Rachel, do this, and hurry up, Rachel, and do that"—but she was an accomplished woman and in the 1930s it was unusual to see a woman running a business. She created it from her own ideas and with the help of her friends who were expert furriers.

Aunt Mary had two daughters, Lois and Enid, who were about my age, but they didn't have to work in her shop like I did. They stayed home with the black maid, who made sure they got plenty of chocolate pudding and Yankee Doodles. I'll never forget that. Yankee Doodles were chocolate-covered cakes with cream inside. I loved them but I couldn't have any. On Sundays the maid would dress Lois and Enid in cute white cotton dresses and those two would stand in the mirror and gawk at each other like two mannequins.

One would say to the other, "Well, dear, you look so nice."

"Thank you, dear."

"Are you ready to go, dear?"

"Why, of course I am, sister."

And off they'd go to the movie theater around the corner, the maid fussing over them as they went. I'd be standing there and they wouldn't even think of asking me to come. If I wanted to tag along, I'd have to pay my own way. I stayed home. See, my mother's family, they didn't say a lot to you. They would always take care of you in a basic way but they never said a lot to you. I didn't feel loved by them. The only one that really loved me was my grandmother, Bubeh. Bubeh loved me. She had moved from Manhattan to an apartment at 1020 President Street in Brooklyn after Zaydeh died. It was near Prospect Park in a building that I believe was owned by my Uncle Dave. Bubeh was a warm, funny woman who spoke no English and was full of life. She was heavy and short, and after she had been here awhile she did away with that wig she wore in Europe and wore her long, shiny white hair combed and twisted into a round bun on the top of her head. She was clean as a whistle. Clean. I mean, she ironed herself to death. Everything she wore was cleaned and ironed. Her cotton housedresses were freshly washed and ironed. Even her tablecloths, which she changed three times a day—when you eat kosher you change the tablecloths for every meal—were ironed and always immaculate. I couldn't iron, you know. I didn't know how to iron a shirt till I got married. I could balance the books at the store and drive a trailer full of supplies and saw wood and pump kerosene and chop ice with an icepick, but I couldn't iron or keep house or cook a pot of grits to save my life and still can't. Boy, your father was in for a shock after he married me.

Bubeh had diabetes and had to take insulin every day, which my Aunt Betsy often gave her. She was on a restricted diet because of her diabetic condition, so we kept a lot of grapefruits and oranges in the house. The oranges were in case she went into a diabetic shock. I was instructed to give her a piece of orange if this happened. I would worry about this constantly, and I'd often sneak into her room when she was taking naps and watch her breathe. If I saw her shake, I'd wake her. "Bubeh! Bubeh!"

"What? What . . ."

"Are you sleeping?" I never knew what to say then.

"Yes, I am sleeping but I can talk as I sleep, it is no problem. Let us talk. What's the matter, Rachel?" She was always so kind. Bubeh took me on my first trolley ride. The trolley used to run down Bergen Street in Brooklyn in those days. It cost five cents and the seats were wooden. You could hang near the back and get an open-air ride. I'd hang my head out the side and let the wind blow in my face, whoooosssssh! Anything that moved I liked. Speed. Trains, trolleys, skates. Bubeh liked to sit on the benches that lined Eastern Parkway near her house and crochet quilts and sweaters and covers for clothes hangers, and chitchat with her Jewish buddies. They were all old women, immigrants who had come over with their children, and America fascinated them. Bubeh often held court talking Yiddish with her pals as people swept past on their way to work. "These young people in America go too fast," she would say—her needle would go zip, zip! while she talked. "My granddaughter, Rachel"—and she'd point to me—

"she can never sit at home. She wants to ride the trolley all day." And the old ladies would nod and smile at me and say, "Yes, yes, but you should stay at home and be a nice girl, Rachel." They were funny old ladies.

My Aunt Betsy, the youngest of my mother's sisters, was living with Bubeh during those early years. She worked as a bookkeeper for a lingerie store on the East Side in Manhattan. Aunt Betts was beautiful, like all of Mameh's sisters. She had long dark hair and dark eyes and dressed fine and took very good care of herself. She had a lot of friends who would drop by the apartment and talk to me and make me feel grown-up. They always talked about shopping at Klein's on Fourteenth Street in Manhattan to pick up dresses at bargain prices. Aunt Betts was young and kind of with it, so when I come up to New York in the summer of '36, pregnant, she could see something was wrong with me. I wasn't showing, but she knew something was going on because I was so distraught. She kept asking me, "What's the matter, Rachel? What's the matter?" I had to tell someone, so I finally broke down and told her. She didn't ask me anything else. She just went about it in that matter-of-fact way my mother's family did things. She made a few phone calls, found a Jewish doctor in Manhattan, and took me to his office, where I had an abortion. It was a horrible, painful experience and the doctor used no anesthesia. Afterwards, I was in so much pain I couldn't walk, so Aunt Betts and I sat on the stoop of the doctor's office and I cried, and even through my tears I was apologizing to her, because I was ashamed. "I'm sorry," I said. "I don't want to be a bother."

"It's all right," Aunt Betts said. "Just don't let it happen again." And that was it.

I was always grateful to Aunt Betts for that. Even though she slammed the door in my face years later, I never felt bitter toward her. She had her own life and her own sets of hurts to deal with, and after all, I wasn't her child. Mameh's sisters were more about money than anything else, and any hurts that popped up along the way, they just swept them under the rug. They were all trying hard to be American, you know, not knowing what to keep and what to leave behind. But you know what happens when you do that. If you throw water on the floor it will always find a hole, believe me.

14.

Chicken Man

For months after my stepfather died, Mommy walked around the house as if she were blind, staggering through the motions of life. She gave away Daddy's clothes, his tools, his hats . . . gone to the Goodwill. She sent us off to school and tried to maintain her crazy house as usual, ranting about this and that, but the fire was gone. In the evening she often sat at the kitchen table completely lost in thought. She'd stop in midsentence and walk away silently, covering her face. At night she cried in her bedroom, though she always hid her tears from us. Daddy's gold Pontiac sat in front of the house for months, leaves gathering around the tires and bird crap gathering on its hood. "I'm going to learn to drive it," she promised, but instead she started riding her bike and taking piano lessons, sitting at the piano every evening, staring at the music and slowly, excruciatingly, picking out the notes to her favorite gospel hymn, "What a Friend We Have in Jesus." She played each note separately, as if they had no connection to each other, and they echoed through the house and landed on the walls like tears. I couldn't stand to hear it. I would cover my ears at night, or better still, I would just go out. There was no one to tell me not to.

My grades plummeted almost immediately. I attended Benjamin Cardozo High School in Bayside, Queens, and while I had been a good student in the ninth grade, the following year I more or less dropped out. I failed everything. I left home in the mornings and simply didn't go to school. Just like Mommy did years before me, I began my own process of running, emotionally disconnecting myself from her, as if by doing so I could keep her suffering from touching me. After years of waiting, I was finally the king in my house, the oldest kid, with the power to boss and torture my younger siblings the way I'd been bossed and tortured, but now that the moment had arrived I spent as much time away from home as possible. I quit church and avoided my deeply religious godparents. I was the first kid on my block to smoke cigarettes and reefer. I joined a soul band, Black Ice, on the other side of town, playing any instrument I could round up— sax, flute, and bass, all borrowed. We played Kool and the Gang songs for hours, smoking weed, drinking Old English 800 malt liquor, and rehearsing in the drummer's basement for days at a time until the guy's mother threw us out, at which time we'd find another place to jam. The band attracted legions of followers—girls, of whom at fourteen I was still deathly afraid, and new friends, cool cats named Beanie, Marvin, Chink, Pig, and Bucky, who smoked cigarettes and reefer, digging the band's sounds. "Oh yeah . . . you can play, man. You are smokin' . . ."

My new friends and I shoplifted. We broke into cars. We snuck onto the nearby Conrail / Long Island Rail Road tracks and broke into freight cars, robbing them of bicycles, television sets, and wine. Once, a cop caught us up there looking to steal but we had no goods on us. He lined us up against a freight car and searched us, then smashed one kid in the face with his blackjack—the kid had tried to say he wasn't with the rest of us. He led us around the freight yards at gunpoint for about an hour, waving his gun under our noses and saying, "You nigger scum. I should shoot you right now." We thought we were going to die, but he let us go. It didn't deter us. At one point we found a freight car so full of wine we stole crates and crates of it. Half the teenagers in St. Albans were wandering around drunk for weeks. The cops tried to crack down and one night caught four of us dividing up cases of the stolen wine on a dead-end street. They rushed in on us, two squad cars with headlights off and cops in the front and back, engines roaring, tires squealing, while we scattered like flies into the junkyard nearby. I barely got away. I was running behind my big slow friend Marvin and couldn't make it to the fence on the other side of the junkyard where everyone else escaped. I dove under an abandoned dump truck and lay quiet, still clasping a bottle of cheap, peppermint-tasting wine in my hand, gritting my teeth, and nearly peeing on myself as I watched the cops' shoes and saw the beam of their flashlights zipping around just inches from my feet. The next day I got so drunk in relief I couldn't make it home. My friend Joe carried me to my house, where I fell down, got up, pissed in the street in front of my sisters, who were desperately trying to get me into the house without Mommy seeing me, then collapsed. When I woke up hours later, Mommy was sitting at the foot of my bed, whipping belt in hand. She whipped me mercilessly, tears in her eyes. It did not help. My friends became my family, and my family and mother just became people I lived with.

I was obviously hiding, and angry as well, but I would never admit that to myself. The marvelous orchestrated chaos that Mommy had so painstakingly constructed to make her house run smoothly broke down when Daddy died, and Mommy was in no fixing mood. My stepfather's final admonition to me went unheeded as I absolved myself of all responsibility and stayed out of the house as much as possible, thus avoiding the emotional impact of watching Mommy suffer. She, in turn, suffered more, having no one to help her keep the younger ones in line. In addition she had no money to pay heating bills, and light bills, and phone bills, sending every dime she had from my stepfather's pension and her small work salary and social security to my siblings in college and grad school. Gradually the house slipped farther and farther into disrepair. I ignored it. To earn dough, I sold reefer, keeping a stash of it at the railroad tracks. When I ran out, I talked my friend Joe into robbing a dealer who we knew had a big stash. Joe had a .22 caliber pistol and I carried a straight-edge shaving razor I'd found among my stepfather's things. We strong-armed the dealer for the weed, and when he protested I hit him and he backed off. When we ran out of dough from that, we snatched a purse on Newburg Street from an old black woman who screamed and hollered while we laughed and ran. We got $1.16 and Joe felt sorry for the woman and refused to do it again, so I did it alone, waiting in the dark doorway of a closed barbershop as the women got off the bus, ripping the purses out of their protesting hands as they cried out in fear and shock. Punk that I was, I did feel sorry for them, their screams echoing in my ears as I ran, my heart beating so hard it felt like a brick pounding against my chest, but not sorry enough. I was numb. I felt I was getting back at the world for injustices I had suffered, but if you sat me down and asked me which injustices I was talking about, I wouldn't have been able to name them if my life depended on it. I snatched old women's purses just as I had seen my own mother's purse snatched when I was eight years old, but in my mind the two acts were not related. I had no feelings. I had smothered them. Every time they surged up, I shoved them back down inside me the way you stuff clothing in a drawer and shut it. Reefer and wine helped me to forget any pain, and as the pain and guilt increased, my problems with drugs worsened.

I took pains to keep my life as a punk a secret from my mother. I stole a bunch of blank report cards from the school library rather than have Ma see my horrible grades, which were basically zero since I never showed up. It was a complicated project requiring real ingenuity and a friend named Vincent, who helped, but I made the mistake of asking my sister Kathy to fill out the one I used for myself, because I was afraid Mommy would recognize my handwriting. Instead of putting down my usual grades—I had been an A student—Kathy wrote in C grades. Mommy looked at the grades and said, "James is no C student." She picked up the phone and called the school and got the shock of her life.

She could not punish me, she knew that. I was too old, too strong, and too far gone. She enrolled me in summer school and I got thrown out. My older brothers came home from college and admonished me, beating me from one end of the house to the other. I still got high and stayed out all hours. Finally Mommy sent me to stay with my sister Jack who had moved from Harlem to Louisville, Kentucky, with her new husband. "Jack will straighten your butt out," she sniffed. I told her I doubted it.

I loved Jack. She was a small, pretty, Christian black woman with freckles and brown eyes that missed nothing. She wore elaborate wigs and talked real down home, with a heavy, deep accent full of "I ain'ts" and "Come owns." She sometimes wrapped her head in scarves and worked as a cook and domestic, usually for white people, but beneath her domestic look was an intelligent, clairvoyant woman who understood more about me as a mixed child than I understood about myself. Jack had lived in Harlem for ten years before moving to Kentucky. She knew more about the street than I did.

Going to stay with Jack for the summer was not punishment for me. It was sweet liberty, and I stayed there three straight summers, always managing to get tossed from summer school in New York City just to get sent down there. Jack was too busy to keep a watchful eye on me, or so I thought. She had a young baby, worked full-time as a cook in a cafeteria, and had a husband who was a handful. The first time I came to her house she told me, "You want to hang out? Go on out, you'll see. But if you come into my house with a gun, I'll shoot you myself," and she meant it. She let me run around, albeit reluctantly, with her husband, Big Richard, whom I worshiped. He was a tall, thin, chocolate-skinned man with a mustache, who favored shades, short-sleeved shirts, shiny shoes, and sharkskin pants, and always held a lit cigarette between his teeth. Big Richard was a cool customer who ran with some rough characters down in Louisville, but while many of his friends had been cut, stabbed, maimed, and shot, Big Richard always stayed injury-free, because his brain worked like a bilge pump, immediately sucking info out of any situation, his mind clicking behind those dark shades at all times. He could walk into a nightclub and sniff danger instantly, backing out right away. "Someone's going to get shot in there," he'd say, and sure enough, the next day you'd hear that someone got tagged.

Richard worked at the Brown and Williamson tobacco plant, but all day and night before his shift started, he and I would go hang out with his boys on "the Corner" at the Vermont Liquor Store, a couple of miles from Jack's house at Thirty-fourth and Vermont Avenue on the city's west side. The three summers I spent at Vermont Liquors on the Corner—which Big Richard pronounced "Coner"—were my true street education.

The men on the Corner were southern working men: plumbers, carpenters, painters, drunks, con artists, retired army lifers from nearby Fort Knox, tobacco workers for Brown and Williamson, and some just plain ol' hustlers. They were big, muscled men with white teeth and huge arms, who wore work clothes and undershirts, painters' pants, and work boots; they smoked filterless Pall Malls and Tareytons and drove big cars—Electra 225's, Cadillacs, and long Oldsmobiles. They liked fine women, good whiskey, crap games, and the local softball league, in which they fielded a team of good-natured alcoholics. They played other teams of good-natured alcoholics, and while fistfights occasionally broke out, rarely was there a gunfight afterwards. The men on the Corner were honorable drinking men, with their own code of ethics: A man's word was his bond, you never insulted anyone's woman, you didn't drink from the same bottle as a man who confessed to oral sex with women, you never cuffed the dice during crap games, and if you pulled out a gun—which you shouldn't do—you'd better use it before it got used on you. They had names like "Red," "Hot Sausage," "One-Armed James," and "Chicken Man," an old drunk who was my favorite.

Chicken Man was a small man with deep, rich, almost copper-toned skin, a wrinkled face, and laughing eyes. He wore an old fishing hat that seemed to cover his entire face, and plaid pants that left about two inches of sock and four inches of ankle showing. He smelled of liquor and beer all the time but he kept a pocket full of candy which he laid on the various children who came by the liquor store to see him, some his kin and some not. You could see him coming from a distance, appearing out of nowhere like an angel, his silhouette seeming to rise from the ground in the simmering heat, though he actually emerged from one of the ramshackle houses that lined the road a half-mile away. He'd stagger up Thirty-fourth Street like a wandering bird lost in flight, his hands spread out at his sides like he was flying, waving at cars that honked at him, arriving on the Corner at two P.M. drunk. He'd set up shop on the Corner like it was his office, sitting in the front of the liquor store on a wood crate and drinking till he ran out of liquor or money, at which time he'd stagger off, blindly drunk, laughing at some silly philosophy he'd just laid down. Chicken Man was a sweet man. He was completely incoherent when he was drunk, but when sober he was one of the chief philosophers of the Corner. He'd sit on his crate like King Tut, his arms folded, his head shaking, and he'd watch traffic pass, commenting on life, liberty, and the pursuit of happiness, money, liquor ("Don't mix corn liquor and cheap wine—ever"), and women ("Never pork a woman on her period—her body's giving off filth"). Chicken Man laughingly called white folks "Mr. Charlie," or "Chuck."

"How Mr. Charlie got his name," Chicken Man explained one day, "is from when you're drunk. You call on him like this: 'Chaaaarrrlll-lieeee.' " He feigned throwing up. "But when you're real, real drunk you call him Chuck, like this: 'Chuuuuccckckckkkkk!,' " He feigned severe throwing up.

"What about Ralph?" I asked, knowing full well that when a dude threw up, we called it ralphing; at least in New York we did.

"Forget Ralph. He don't count. Mr. Charlie counts. Now buy me a beer."

The men on the Corner seemed to pay no attention to Mr. Charlie. The closest they came to him was when the police rode by, sometimes stopping to ask if anyone had seen this or that person. They were met with stony silence, or sometimes even jokes and laughter.

The men did not seem to be afraid of the police, nor did they dislike them. Their lives just seemed complete without the white man. I liked that. Their world was insular, away from the real world that I was running from. They called me "New York," and let me sit out there all day, practicing my flute and smoking all the weed I wanted. I turned fifteen on the Corner but could act like I was twenty-five, and no one cared. I could hide. No one knew me. No one knew my past, my white mother, my dead father, nothing. It was perfect. My problems seemed far, far away.

One of Big Richard's good friends was a guy named Pike, who had dark skin, a moustache and an easygoing manner. I stole a few car batteries with Pike until somebody saw us in their driveway at night, flicked the porch light on, and took a potshot at us. "You don't need to be doing this no way," Pike said, panting for breath when we were in the clear. He wouldn't let me run with him anymore after that. Like most dudes on the Corner, he looked out for me. When I protested, saying I needed money, he said, "Don't worry. I'm gonna get you a job in a turd factory, making all the money you want."

"What's a turd factory?" I asked.

"It's a factory where they make turds." He explained this to me one afternoon while he, Big Richard, and I were cruising around in his car. Big Richard was riding shotgun, chomping on his cigarette, and staring out the window to keep from laughing.

"I want the job," I said. "What do I do?"

"You sit in a big chair and the turds float down this long stream of water, and you separate the big turds from the little turds."

"How do you do that?"

"They got a tool you use. Or you can use your hand. Whatever. It don't matter. It's good money, man! You want the job or not?"

"I want it, man! I want the job! Take me there!"

I finally did get a real job pumping gas at a station about a mile from the Corner. The man who ran it was named Herman, a big, burly black man with a wide chest who was mean as the day was long. My first day on the job, the mechanic at the station, a young light-skinned black guy, told me, "Don't cross Herman. He put two men down already." I didn't ask any questions about those two cats, just made sure I wasn't the third, because Herman was a big, mean, irritated, angry, butt-kicking dude. Every night just before closing time he'd hand me a bucket full of gas and a mop and say, "Mop this god-dam floor and don't smoke while you doin' it neither." Then he'd stand right outside the door and smoke and watch me mop the entire floor of the auto shop. Nobody ever robbed Herman's station while I was there, nor did any customers ever fool with him.

My job was to pump gas, change tires, fix flats, and generally keep out of Herman's way, which I more or less did, but I got into a fist-fight with one of his friends, a scar-faced, scratch-a-match-in-the-palm-of-his-hand homosexual who was harassing me. Who knows, maybe it was my girly face and New York accent, but he got funky with me one afternoon and I punched him in the face a few times be-fore he went under his car seat for his pistol and chased me around the station. The ruckus caused a big stir and Herman fired me on the spot. I retreated to the Corner, plotting revenge and seeking wisdom from my main man, Chicken Man. A sober Chicken Man had two words of advice. "Forget it," he said.

"I can't forget it. I should've gotten a gun and shot him," I said.

Chicken Man chuckled. "You don't know shit from Shinola," he said. "Is that how you want to end up, goin' to jail for him? Because that's where you'll end up, doing time and hanging on this corner when you get out. Is that what you want for yourself? 'Cause if you do, you can have it. Go on."

"I'm a smart guy," I said. "I don't have to take that kind of shit. Nobody knows how smart I really am, Chicken Man, but I'm smart."

"And nobody'll give a damn neither!" Chicken Man snapped. "Everybody on this corner is smart. You ain't no smarter than anybody here. If you so smart, why you got to come on this corner every summer? 'Cause you flunkin' school! You think if you drop out of school somebody's gonna beg you to go back? Hell no! They won't beg your black ass to go back. What makes you so special that they'll beg you! Who are you? You ain't nobody! If you want to drop out of school and shoot people and hang on this corner all your life, go ahead. It's your life!"

I had never heard Chicken Man talk so severely and what he said didn't really hit me, not right away. I said to myself, "He's just a drunk," and continued my adventures. Not long after, however, a guy named Mike, an easygoing, humorous six-foot-eight guy who had always encouraged me to get off the street, had an argument on the Corner with his girlfriend Mustang, a fine, lithe black woman with a large black ass and a foxy wiggle. As the argument progressed, Mike began slapping Mustang around so hard I wanted to jump in, but Chicken Man stopped me. "Leave that alone, New York!" he hissed. "That's between him and his woman. Don't never get between a man and his woman." Mustang left the corner in her car, burning rubber, promising to bring her new boyfriend back to kill Mike. The Corner quickly emptied—there was nothing like the threat of a gunfight to make everyone go home. The next day Big Richard gave me explicit instructions to "stay off the Corner," but I snuck over there anyway and watched as Mike came by that afternoon, rumbling up in his big Buick, playing Marvin Gaye on his eight-track player. He cut the engine and got out whistling, totally cooled out, like it was another day at the office. He walked to the back of his car, opened the trunk, and calmly pulled out a lawn chair, a towel, and a sawed-off double-barreled shotgun with both barrels taped together. He set the lawn chair in front of the store and sat down on it. He put a bottle of J&B scotch on the ground on one side of him, a bottle of Boone's Farm Strawberry Hill wine on the other side, placed the shotgun on his lap, and put the towel over it. "I'm gonna set here and drink and rock and I'll wait for him," he said coolly. He sat there for two days, rocking, drinking, while the men tiptoed around him, keeping one eye on the road and one eye on Mike. Mustang's new boyfriend never showed.

The next week, Mike and Mustang showed up on the Corner arm in arm, kissing and hugging.

"That's why I don't have no arguments with no woman," Chicken Man said. "It don't do nothing but fool you around." But not long after, he did get into an argument with a woman. They argued in the morning and he went off and forgot about it, and later that day she came into the liquor store and stabbed him as he was waiting in line to buy a beer. He coughed a few times, then lay down on the floor and died.

15.

Graduation

After my abortion I wrote to Tateh and said I didn't want to come back to Suffolk. I enrolled in Girls Commercial High School on Bergen Street in 1936. It was just down the street from Bubeh's, but the schoolwork was hard and I struggled my entire junior year, sleeping on Bubeh's couch and wrestling with algebra every night. Girls High was way ahead of Suffolk High and I never would've graduated on time, so after the school year ended I returned to Virginia to finish high school. When I came back to Suffolk, the first thing I said to Peter was, "We can't see each other anymore. Don't come by."

He said, "I've been waiting for you. I still love you," and I was swayed, because I still felt a deep love for him.

Not long after that, I was in the store behind the counter and two young black women came in. I overheard them talking about Peter, and one of them says, "Oh yeah, he's getting married soon . . ." I almost fell over. Tateh was standing right next to me, so I grabbed a rag and started wiping the counter, edging close to them, eavesdropping. I was practically falling over the counter trying to hear them. "Oh yeah," says the other. "He got such and such pregnant . . ." She named a black girl who lived behind us in the neighborhood.

I went right out and found him. The heck with who knew about us then. I was so mad I marched right down the road to his house in daylight and got him out. "Tell me the truth," I said. He confessed it. "They're making me marry her," he said. "My folks are making me."

"Did you get her pregnant?"

"Yeah."

Oh, that messed me up. I told him I didn't want to see him anymore and walked back through the black neighborhood, into the store, and went upstairs and cried my heart out, because I still loved him. I went through this entire ordeal and here he was getting busy with somebody else. The fact that he was black and the girl he was marrying was black—well, that hurt me even more. If the world were fair, I suppose I would have married him, but there was no way that could happen in Virginia. Not in 1937.

I made up my mind then that I was going to leave Suffolk for good. I was seventeen, in my last year of high school, and for the first time in my life I was starting to have opinions of my own. There was no life for me there. I was planning to leave for New York. But see, I had Mameh. I was her eyes and ears in America. She couldn't speak English and I translated for her and looked out for her, because Tateh didn't care for her at all. Her stomach was starting to bother her and she was starting to have these fainting spells, you know, she'd just black out in the middle of the day. Tateh couldn't have cared less. He hired a black woman to look after Mameh and that woman cared for Mameh more than he did. She'd stay late and look after Mameh even if he didn't pay her, and he paid her so little as it was. He thought money he spent to take care of his wife would do it, you know, substitute for the fact that he didn't love her. But a wife wants love. She was a good Jewish wife to him, but their marriage was starting to crumble because he didn't care about her. That's why I knew I was leaving home. I wasn't going to have an arranged marriage like my parents did. I'd rather die first, which I did do in a way, because I lost my mother and sister when I left home.

Well, the kids in my high school were excited and giggling about the prom and graduation and making plans, but I'd been to New York and seen the big time and didn't plan on going to either. No one asked me to the prom anyway, but Frances kept saying, "Please go to graduation, Ruth. We'll walk together on graduation day." I never told Frances about any of that business I was going through. None of that stuff about Peter and my abortion in New York. She knew my home life wasn't perfect, but Frances wasn't the type to question you. She was just a giving, kind person. So I decided to go to the graduation ceremony for her, because Frances was my best friend and I would do anything for her.

Suffolk High had this graduation ceremony where the seniors lined up in their caps and gowns outside the high school and marched onto Main Street double file to the Protestant church for a ceremony. They called it a pre-graduation ceremony or baccalaureate or some such thing. I had to ask Tateh for money for the cap and gown, and the minute he heard about me marching into a Protestant church, he said, "No. Forget it. You're not marching into any gentile church." He was dead set against it. You know my parents were so old-fashioned European in their ways it wasn't funny. Like if you took a social worker into my house and he talked to my parents, it would be like talking to that wall over there. They were stuck in their ways. There was no way they could change. He was still my father, and I was still a teenager living in his house, and he could still pull off his belt and beat the mess out of me when he wanted, so what could I do? He wasn't worried about my graduation. What bothered him more was that I had no marriage prospects, and he began to take me on his business jaunts to Portsmouth and Norfolk, around to the stores and wholesale supply houses, and he'd introduce me to the merchants and their sons if they had any. It was like he was saying, "Here's my daughter on display! What do you think?" Sometimes he'd send me on jaunts by myself, driving the car and pulling the trailer, me and Dee-Dee. We'd load *up the trailer full of goods from the warehouses and drive though the Dismal Swamp around Portsmouth and Norfolk. Folks would tell us, "Watch out for the red-light district in Norfolk," and we'd go around Norfolk avoiding red traffic lights.*

Well, I was upset with Tateh about graduation and we weren't speaking for a while, but he'd reached a point where he really needed me to help him run the store, because Sam was gone and Mameh wasn't feeling well. Her stomach was starting to really bother her, to the point where she'd be doubled over in pain. We'd take her to the town doctor and he'd say this or that. He mentioned an operation of some sort, but he didn't know. He was a nasty old man. I went to him once and he was as fresh as he could be, touching me in places that were not necessary and saying obscene things, so I never went back to him. Of course I couldn't tell anybody about it. But he looked at Mameh and said he didn't know what was wrong with her.

Well, Tateh and I argued about the cap and gown for a long time, and at one point I got so mad I revealed my plans to go to New York after graduation. "I'm going back to New York," I told him. "I'm leaving." He stalked out the room, cursing and swearing. A few minutes later, Mameh followed him out and spoke to him—they were rarely speaking by then—and the next day he came over and gave me the money for my cap and gown. "You can participate in the march," he said, "but don't go into that church. It's forbidden."

"I'm going to the ceremony," I said.

"Respect your mother and me," he said. "Don't break the law of the Bible. Don't go into that gentile church," he said.

Well, my mind was made up.

On graduation day Dee-Dee and I opened up the store, set out the meats, stacked the fresh vegetables, and I worked behind the counter until it was time to go. Of course my parents wouldn't go to that gentile graduation, so I put on my cap and gown and walked the six blocks to Suffolk High School alone and waited for Frances in the parking lot. Frances was late getting there, which gave the other students and their parents something to stare at, to watch me standing there by myself. I was ready to turn around and run home by the time she showed up. I told her, "Frances, I'm not sure I can go into that church." She said, "I understand, Ruth. I'll graduate by myself, then, because I don't want to graduate next to anyone but you." Well, I felt like I couldn't let that happen, so I said, "I can do it, let's go." We took a picture in our caps and gowns and got in line, double file, and marched together. The line marched out of Suffolk High's schoolyard and onto Main Street and slowed as it bottled up at the church doorway. As we approached the church I started to shake and sweat, and just before we reached the church doorway, I stepped out of line. I couldn't do it. I just couldn't go inside that church. In my heart I was still a Jew. I had done some wrong things in my life, but I was still my parents' child.

I turned away, but not before Frances saw my tears. She got out of line herself but I waved her away. "Frances, you go on in," I said. "Don't miss the ceremony because of me." She went in. She had to wipe the tears from her own face, but she got back in line and marched through the ceremony alone, and she sat through the graduation ceremony next to my empty seat.

I walked home sobbing in my cap and gown and caught a Greyhound bus for New York the very next day.

16.

Driving

One Saturday morning in 1973, a few weeks after I got back from Louisville, and just a few months after my stepfather passed away, Mommy woke me up and said, "We're going driving." She thrust my two-year-old niece Z—that was her name, just plain Z—into my arms and we headed out to Daddy's car.

My stepfather had kept his '68 Pontiac Catalina, gold-colored with blue interior, immaculate. Before that he'd had a '65 Chevy Impala that he paid good money for. The car, white with red interior, was a bomb. He called it "a cheesebox. I'll never buy another Chevy again," he fumed as the car, loaded with kids, sat in traffic, its engine steaming and sputtering. It seemed to break down every five minutes.

When it did start, a key wasn't necessary. You simply turned the ignition switch with your hand and it fired, and one evening a guy did just that as Daddy was standing by the kitchen window washing dishes. He watched in silence as the guy drove off in a cloud of blue smoke. "This must be my lucky day," he said.

Mommy had never driven before as far as I knew. She was afraid to drive. She was a certified dyed-in-the-wool New York City transit passenger who could tell you what subway train went anywhere, which stop to get off at, and how far it was to the next one if you missed your stop and had to walk back. Depending on public transporation meant she was late for everything—for work, for open school nights, for picking us up whenever she had to. Every summer when I returned home from Fresh Air Fund camp, the yellow school buses would drop us off in Manhattan and I'd mournfully watch three hundred hugging, kissing, slobbering happy reunions between campers and parents while the counselors flipped coins to see who would wait with me, at which time Mommy would finally turn the corner at Forty-second Street—I could spot her bowed legs a mile away—and run up breathlessly, hugging me as the counselors looked on with looks that said, "I had no idea!"

But those days were gone. We needed a car. It was time for Mommy to drive. "I hate this," she said, as we climbed in. "You have to tell me what to do." I was almost sixteen then and though I had no license I knew how to drive, having spent a good deal of time driving Daddy's car when Ma wasn't around, not to mention other cars I wasn't supposed to be driving. How she knew I knew how to drive she mercifully chose not to discuss, but by then I had begun to turn around. Deep inside I knew that my old friend Chicken Man back in Louisville was right. I wasn't any smarter, or any wiser, or any bolder than the cats on the Corner, and if I chose that life I would end up on the Corner no matter what my brains or potential. I knew I wasn't raised to drink every day, to work at a gas station, and to get killed fooling around with people like Herman and his gas station knuckle-heads. That life wasn't as wild and as carefree as it looked from the outside anyway. It was ragged and cruel and I didn't want to end up that way, stabbed to death after an argument over a bottle of wine, or shot dead by some horny dude who was trying to take my manhood. "You have to choose between what the world expects of you and what you want for yourself," my sister Jack told me several times. "Put your-self in God's hands and you can't go wrong." I knew Jack was right, and when I got back to New York in the fall of 1973 for my junior year in high school I resolved to jump back into my studies and re-build myself. Like my own mother did in times of stress, I turned to God. I lay in bed at night praying to Him to make me strong, to rid me of anger, to make me a man, and He listened, and I began to change.

I didn't change right away. For one thing, I was still strung out on herb. I'd watch newscasters Roger Grimsby and a young Geraldo Rivera do grim-faced reports on Channel 7 *Eyewitness News* about the dangers of being "hooked" on marijuana and I'd laugh. "You can't get hooked on reefer," I told my friends. "I can stop anytime I want." But deep inside, I knew I was hooked, and I was secretly jealous of those from my drug circle who got themselves together and pulled out. Day after day I found myself in some dude's house getting blasted on weed and alcohol while he stuffed towels under the door to keep the smell in. I was also suffering occasional flashbacks from taking LSD, which I had done a lot the previous year. The flashbacks came out of nowhere: a joint or cigarette would set them off, or nothing at all—I'd be walking down the street and suddenly find myself blasted, tripping, that acid clairvoyancy high where people seem to be made of glass and the back of your hand becomes a purple star. I'd wander around the neighborhood paranoid, avoiding everyone I knew until the high wore off. Thank God crack wasn't available then, because I would've certainly become a crack addict. As it was, every single day—on the way to school, during school, and on the way home—I felt I had to get high. If I ran out of pot I drank wine, and when I couldn't get that my buddy Marvin and I drank NyQuil, which got you high and sleepy and slightly sick. I'd come home every night blasted, smelling like a pot house, promising myself as I put my key in the door that I wouldn't get high the next day, only to open it and find Mommy standing behind it, screaming at me, "What's the matter with you! Your eyes are all red and you smell funny!" I wanted to give up weed, but I couldn't. Weed was my friend, weed kept me running from the truth. And the truth was my mother was falling apart.

Looking back, I see it took about ten years for Mommy to recover from my stepfather's death. It wasn't just that her husband was suddenly gone, it was the accumulation of a lifetime of silent suffering, some of which my siblings and I never knew about. Her past had always been a secret to us, and remained so even after my stepfather died, but what she had left behind was so big, so complete that she could never entirely leave it: the dissipation of her own Jewish family, the guilt over abandoning her mother, the separation from her sister, the sudden, tragic death of her first husband, whom she adored. While she never seemed on the verge of losing her mind, there were moments when she teetered close to the edge, lost in space. Even in my own self-absorbed funk, I was worried about her, because as my siblings and I slowly got to our emotional feet, Mommy staggered about in an emotional stupor for nearly a year. But while she weebled and wobbled and leaned, she did not fall. She responded with speed and motion. She would not stop moving. She rode her bicycle. She

walked. She took long bus rides to faraway department stores and supermarkets where she'd window-shop for hours and spend fifty cents.
She could not grasp exactly what to do next, but she kept moving as if
her life depended on it, which in some ways it did. She ran, as she had
done most of her life, but this time she was running for her own
sanity.

She operated on automatic mode, rising each morning and chasing us off to school as if things were as they always were, but she
could make no decisions. Even the simplest choice, like whether to
have a Touch-Tone telephone or a rotary one, required enormous,
painstaking deliberation. If the furnace broke down it stayed broken,
not just because she didn't have the money to fix it, but because . . .
well . . . just because. She had always been incredibly disorganized,
but now her disorganization reached new heights. I went to gym
class, opened a paper bag from home in which I had stored my gym
gear, and found her underwear inside. She'd disappear from the house
for hours and come back with no explanation as to where she'd been.
About a year after my stepfather died, her best friend, a wonderful
black woman named Irene Johnson, passed away and Mommy
teetered at the edge again, standing over the kitchen sink washing the
same pot for hours, sniffling back her tears, and snapping, "Get away
from me!" when we approached her. "You only have one or two good
friends in life," she used to preach at us, and for her, Irene was one of
those. She and Irene went back to Harlem in the forties when Ma
first came to New York. Irene understood how far she had come.
Irene had helped her raise her older children and had been like a sister to her. Yet she refused to go to Irene's memorial service. "I'm
done with funerals," she announced, yet you could see the pain on
her face as she picked up the phone to dial Irene's sister to ask her
about the final details of her best friend's life. "Please stay in touch,"

Ma said, and Irene's sister did, for years. Ma was utterly confused about all but one thing: Jesus. The young Jewish girl who at one time could not allow herself to walk into a gentile church now couldn't do without it; her Orthodox Jewish ways had long since translated themselves into full-blown Christianity. Jesus gave Mommy hope. Jesus was Mommy's salvation. Jesus pressed her forward. Each and every Sunday, no matter how tired, depressed, or broke, she got up early, dressed in her best, and headed for church. When we kids grew too old and big for her to force us to go, she went alone, riding the F train from Queens to Brooklyn to New Brown Memorial, the church she started with my father. Church revived her, filled her up, and each Sunday she returned a little more renewed, until that Saturday afternoon she announced she was going to drive my step-father's car.

She sat behind the wheel, tapping it nervously and muttering while I settled in the front seat and held Z in my arms. We didn't bother with seat belts. She stuck the key in the ignition. The engine roared to life. "What do you do now?" she asked.

"Put it in gear," I said.

"Oh, I know that," she said. She slammed the car into drive and pulled off in a cloud of burning rubber and smoke, swerving down the street, screaming hysterically—Woooooooooo!"

"Slow down, Ma!" I said.

She ignored me. "I don't have a license!" she shrieked as the car veered from side to side. "If I get stopped I'm going to jail!" She went about four blocks, ran a stop sign without pausing, then at the next intersection whipped a wide, arcing left turn, stabbing the accelerator pedal and sending the big sedan reeling down the wrong side of the street as oncoming traffic swerved to avoid us.

"Watch it! What are you doing, Ma! Stop the car!" I hollered.

"I need to go to the A&P! I need to go to the A&P!" she shrieked. "This is what I'm driving for, right?" We jerked along for a few blocks, no cops anywhere, and miraculously arrived at the A&P. Since she didn't know how to parallel-park next to the curb, she pulled up next to a parked car, slammed on the brakes, put the car in park, smashed the parking brake with her foot, and got out, leaving the engine running. "Wait here," she said. I held Z in my arms while Mommy ran inside. When she came back out she released the parking brake, threw the car into drive, and pulled away without looking over her shoulder. Then suddenly, for no apparent reason—she might have gotten the accelerator and the brake pedal mixed up—she stood on the brake pedal with all her might. The power brakes locked and I was thrown toward the windshield with little Z in my arms. The baby's tiny head flew at the dashboard with a great whipping motion, missing it by a millimeter. Had she hit it, the force would have severely injured her. The car sat there, the motor humming softly, while Mommy gasped for breath. "That's it," she said. "I quit." She drove home slowly, parked the car, and walked away from it like she had never seen it in her life. She never got inside it again. It sat there for months, leaves gathering around its tires again, snow accumulating on its hood, till she finally sold it. "I'll never learn to drive," she said.

The irony was that Mommy knew how to drive before she was eighteen. She drove her father's 1936 Ford back in Suffolk, Virginia. Not only did she drive it, she drove it well enough to pull a trailer behind it full of wholesale supplies for her family's grocery store. She drove the car and trailer on paved and dirt roads between Norfolk, Suffolk, Portsmouth, Virginia Beach, and North Carolina. She could back the trailer up with the goods in it, unload it at the store, back the car into the yard, unhook the trailer, and park the car in the garage, backing in. But she had left her past so far behind that she literally did not know how to drive. Rachel Deborah Shilsky could drive a car and pull a trailer behind it, but Ruth McBride Jordan had never touched a steering wheel before that day in 1973, and you can make book on it.

17.

Lost in Harlem

When I came to New York after high school, I worked in my Aunt Mary's leather factory and stayed with Bubeh, who had moved to the Bronx. It wasn't a good situation. I wasn't a child anymore. My mother's sisters were done with me. Aunt Mary let me work in her factory, but she cut me no slack by any means. By then she was an obese woman with a very pretty face, and she ruled her whole roost with an iron fist, including Uncle Isaac, her husband. What a henpecked husband he was. He was a shoemaker who worked at an exclusive shoe factory at Fifty-third and Fifth Avenue—H. Bendel's. They stitched shoes for some of the richest women in New York, movie stars like Janet Gaynor and Myrna Loy. I thought he had the most glorious job in the world, meeting movie stars, but I was scared of him. He was a balding man with a nervous twitch in his face and he drank heavily as soon as he walked in the house. He always hid a bottle of liquor in the kitchen cabinet and he'd take big swigs from it and lean on the counter, breathing heavily. His face would turn red and he'd become vulgar and mean.

Meanwhile his wife, Aunt Mary, was having her own party with a man named Mr. Stein. He was her best friend's husband. What a scandal. That man was fine too, honey! Yes he was! Tall and handsome. He'd come into her factory office twice a week and they'd close the door, smooch it up, and have wine and cheese and crackers. I knew this because I was the one Aunt Mary sent to the store for their refreshments. She'd snap, "Rachel! Go get me some wine and cheese and crackers!" and sure enough, after a while up jumps ol' Mr. Stein. He'd slip into her office so they could close the door and smooch away. After an hour or two Aunt Mary would come out with her hair and makeup all mussed up and her face all red. Of course I acted like I saw none of this. I was happy to get a job.

Shortly after I got there, around 1939, she hired a new man who had just come to New York from North Carolina named Andrew McBride. He called himself by his middle name, Dennis. That was your father. Now that was a true man there. By that I mean he was inquisitive, and funny, and easygoing and secure. Dennis was an excellent leathermaker and artisan type and he quickly became Aunt Mary's best worker. Aunt Mary liked to boss all her workers around, and one day she told Dennis to pick up a huge roll of leather and take it to Manhattan by subway. The roll weighed nearly a hundred pounds. Dennis said, "I'm sorry, but it's impossible for one person to carry that alone," and he refused to do it. That was one of the first times I ever saw a man, any man, stick up to Aunt Mary. She backed down.

Dennis saw the callous way my aunt treated me, and he saw her love trysts with Mr. Stein, and he never said anything about how she acted with Mr. Stein, but he'd always offer a kind word to me, or just make a joke. What a sense of humor he had. That man could make a dog laugh. He'd sometimes bring me a cup of coffee or just do kind things for people. Not just for me, but for anyone. That's the kind of person he was. He was the kindest man I'd ever met to this day, and if I'd had any sense I would've snatched him up right away and married him. But I was young and trying to get away from my family and plus I discovered Harlem.

I don't know what drew me there—maybe because I'd lived around black folks most of my life, or because I'd heard so much about it. In those days, nobody in New York City went to the Village to have fun. Harlem was the place. White and black came to Harlem to party. There weren't heavy drugs and crime like there is now. It was different. People were flowing up to Harlem in droves, from the South, from Chicago, from everyplace. Harlem was like magic.

I'd take the number 2 subway train from Aunt Mary's factory and jump off at 125th Street and the adventure would begin. There were theaters from Eighth Avenue down to Lenox Avenue. One block of Harlem had more movie theaters than all of Suffolk: the Loew's, the Alhambra, the Rialto, then crossing over onto Seventh Avenue were a bunch of smaller theaters, and of course on 125th Street you had the Apollo Theater. Sometimes I'd go into the Apollo and stay all afternoon. There were four shows and if you went in at eleven A.M. you could see three shows—plus the movies. I got tired of Aunt Mary treating me so mean, so I quit her factory and started looking for a job as an usher or movie ticket clerk in Harlem. I'd always liked movies and theaters, so one afternoon I moseyed up to this movie house on Seventh Avenue and asked for the manager. He came out, looked at me, and asked, "What the heck are you doing in Harlem?"

"I'm looking for a job," I said.

"What kind of job do you want?" he asked.

"A ticket clerk," I said.

"What else are you looking for?" he asked.

"I'm not looking for anything else," I said. "I want a job as a ticket clerk. Or an usher. You have an usher job?" He got mad. "We don't do that kind of thing here," he said. "You got to go somewhere else to do that," he said. I never caught on to what he was saying. This man thought I was a prostitute, which I almost did become. I went to a few other places with similar results. Nobody would hire me. Why would a white girl hang around Harlem unless she was up to something bad? When there was so much work downtown? Impossible! And I was so naive I just kept wandering around, not knowing I was headed for trouble, which I found soon enough.

I had no luck with movie theaters, so I decided to try beauty parlors. Back in Suffolk, Tateh made me take a beauty course from a woman who had a thriving beauty parlor downtown. She employed one beautician, a blond girl who wore orange lipstick and lived out in the country and came into Suffolk every day to work. This girl taught me how to do manicures and also to work on hair: how to finger-wave, shampoo, and give permanents—but this was on white people's hair. Well, I said, "Hair is hair," and I went into a little place off 135th and Seventh Avenue and said, "I can give permanents," and the woman hired me and gave me a chair. Well, I didn't know a thing about perming black people's hair and my first customer was a black woman and I mauled that woman's hair. Her hair looked like chopped meat when I was done. I kept telling her, "You'll be ready as a radio, ready as a radio." That was a big saying back then, "ready as a radio." I told her this while I was perming and cutting her hair, because when you're a hairdresser you have to chat with the customers and make them feel good and act like everything is toasty. Well, I didn't last the day before they threw me out.

I fumbled around, fumbled around, and finally I said to myself, "Well, I can manicure good." I'd seen plenty salons and barbershops with signs posted that said, "Manicurist Wanted." These were mostly men's barbershops. That didn't bother me because I heard that being a manicurist in a barbershop was easy and the tips were good. I walked up and down Seventh Avenue and finally I came to a place called the Hi Hat Barbershop. It was a block from Small's Paradise on Seventh Avenue and 138th Street. There was a sign in the window that said "Manicurist Wanted," so I went in and inquired about the job.

The manager, Rocky, was a heavy, well-dressed, light-skinned man with a deep voice. He was in his fifties. He hired me immediately. He put the manicuring table in the front window and he plopped me right there and I worked in the window. I went home that night and told my grandmother I had a job that paid fifteen dollars per week. Bubeh said, "What kind of job is it?"

"It's a good job," I told her, but I didn't tell her what kind of job it was, and neither did I tell her where it was. There were a lot of entertainers and musicians who came through there and many times I heard them remark to the boss, "Rocky, you're *taking a chance having this underage white girl working here." But he didn't pay them no mind. I was nineteen and that was old enough for him. He began to hang around my manicure table all the time. One day he told me he would take me to lunch and I accepted. He had a nice car parked in front of the shop, and he was quite prosperous, so I went out with him.*

I didn't make too much of it. I wasn't aware that he had other plans for me. He started taking me out more and more, to the Apollo and movies, and then he would drive me home to the Bronx. He had a nice car and money, so what the heck. I was impressed by that. He took me to clubs and he was well known to folks there. Sometimes he would take me into Small's Paradise, which was frequented by musicians, entertainers, pimps, and prostitutes, and he seemed to know everyone. I told him I always wanted to be a dancer, that I wanted to try for the Rockettes at Radio City. He said, "I'll set it up," but I got scared and didn't go to the audition. I was a dumb small-town girl, but I wasn't dumb enough to go down there and make a fool of myself. What if all the other girls danced better than me? Forget it, honey.

Rocky rented me a room on 122nd near Seventh so I wouldn't have to make that long trip to my grandmother's house in the Bronx. He took me driving down Seventh Avenue, and up and down 125th Street. There were girls standing around in the street. He said, "I'm going to teach you about those girls soon." Well, I knew what was happening then, but I didn't say anything. I didn't have any objection to it at first.

I would stay in the little room he rented for me for a few days, then go back to Bubeh's, then go back there to my little room again. Bubeh was getting very suspicious now, but she was very old then, she slept a lot, you know, and she had diabetes, and I got over on her the way my grandkids get over on me now. I told her anything, you know, and after a while it got so that I couldn't see my grandmother anymore and keep doing what I was doing, hanging out in Harlem. I had to break away and not go back home to her, because Bubeh reminded me too much of what I was and where I came from. I needed to move into Harlem completely and make enough money to stay there and be cool and wear the fancy dresses and the clothes. So one day I asked Rocky, "When do I get to make money like your other girls?" I knew what I was saying. I wasn't blind. But what was love to me? What did I know about love? And sex? I wanted to be swinging, but Rocky said, "You're not ready to get out there yet. I'll tell you when you're ready."

Well, one night I was fooling around up at Small's Paradise or one of those clubs with Rocky, and I hadn't been back to Bubeh's for a couple of weeks, and for some reason I started thinking about Mameh and Dee-Dee. I was afraid to call home because of Tateh, but I knew Dennis was working for Aunt Mary, so I somehow ran him down in Harlem where he was staying. I asked him to see if he could find out how my mother and sister were doing, because it was a small factory, and he would hear my aunt talking about things. He said, "They've been looking for you, Ruth. How are you doing?" and I told him all about my new flat and my new friend Rocky and how nice he was, and a look crossed Dennis's face that just made me go silent.

I was living high off the hog, you know, just trying to bury my past and get away from my father, but when I started to tell Dennis what I was doing, I felt so ashamed, because the look on his face said it all.

He said, "Ruth, your parents haven't done nothing to you that was so bad as to make you run around with that man. That man's a pimp. He's a pimp and he's leading you around by the nose." And he sat there and he kind of fumed. He wasn't angry. He just seemed disappointed.

I felt so ashamed then. I got up and said, "They don't have to look for me anymore. I'm going home." I gathered myself together and went straight back to Bubeh's in the Bronx. She was so worried about me, but when she asked where I'd been I didn't give her direct answers. I just told her not to answer any phone calls or give out any kind of communication about me. Rocky called and sent flowers but I never called him back. He was persistent and at one point came to Bubeh's apartment and knocked on the door and stood in the hallway saying, "Come out, Ruth. I know you're home. Come on out." But I stood behind the door and didn't open it or say a word. He kept sending flowers and trying to get me back into his clutches, but after a while he stopped calling and I never saw him again.

18.

Lost in Delaware

In June 1974, Mommy walked into the kitchen of our house in Queens and said, "We're moving to Delaware. Pack up the house." She had five kids at home and seven who were away at college. Some were in graduate school, some in medical school. All had scholarships or loans and were barely making it themselves, and thus could not help her financially. Our house had fallen into tremendous disrepair and Mommy couldn't keep up with it any longer.

We packed up the house for weeks. I was ready to move. If we stayed in New York, it was almost certain I'd have to do an extra year of high school to finish. Plus I kept running into my old friends, who were getting into bigger and bigger trouble. I needed to see some new faces, a fresh start. My younger sisters, on the other hand, loved living in New York, had none of my problems, and didn't want to leave. "Why move?" they argued. "We're happy here." They called a family meeting. Mommy sat down to talk it out, listened to their reasoning, pursed her lips, and nodded her head. "If you feel that way," she said, "we'll stay." She got up and announced breezily, "We're not moving," and walked out of the room. It was as if she had pulled out a grenade, yanked the pin, dropped it on the floor, and exited. My brothers and I looked at one another in shock. By then the house had been on the market and was being sold. There was a buyer. Contracts had been signed. Teachers had been told. Preparations had been made. We argued about it for hours. "We should move," I said.

"Forget it," my sisters argued.

"We have to go," my older brothers commanded. They felt Ma couldn't afford to live in New York any longer.

Ma was called in to reenter the debate. "Let me think about it again," she said. She sat down on the couch and immediately dropped off to sleep, snoring away while the rest of us argued. My mother is the only individual I know who can fall asleep instantly for two minutes—deep REM sleep, complete with snoring—only to be awakened instantly by certain select noises. A hurricane won't move her, but the sound of a crying baby or a falling pot will send her to her feet like a soldier at reveille. When she awoke, she wandered off saying nothing. Days passed. Finally she announced: "We're staying." Cheers from the girls. We slowly began to unpack. The very next day she barked: "We're moving!" Cheers from the boys. We packed again. Ma went back and forth on this for weeks while the realtor pulled out his hair trying to decide if his commission was going to come through or not. The debate lasted literally up to the August morning when we rented a U-Haul truck, loaded it up with all our worldly possessions—some of us riding with the furniture in the back—and pointed it down I-95 toward Wilmington, Delaware, looking like the Beverly Hillbillies. "Why Wilmington?" we asked Ma.

"Why not?" she said. "It's cheap." She had bought a small house in town for less than twelve thousand dollars, which is what she could afford.

We knew nothing about Delaware. Mommy had an old friend from Harlem who lived there. "You'll do fine in Delaware," Ma's friend said, but from the moment we parked our U-Haul in front of our new home we were completely lost.

We thought we'd function in Wilmington as we had in New York, catching subways and buses and living off public transportation and the groove of the city. But Wilmington had no subway and only the very poor took the bus, which stopped running at about nine P.M. Unlike New York, where Ma could stretch a dollar for a mile and lead her troops to the promised land of Macy's, Gimbels, and Ohrbach's, entertaining them for free at museums, parades, block parties, and public concerts, Wilmington was a land of suburban shopping malls, high school marching bands, blond prom queens, small-town gossip, and an inner city from which whites were fleeing as fast as their Ford Pintos could take them. We were shocked by the racial division of the city and surrounding county, where most of the black kids attended understaffed and underfunded city schools while whites attended sparkling clean suburban schools with fantastic facilities. The segregated schools came as a complete surprise to Mommy, who had not even considered that problem, and the southern vibe of the city— anything south of Canal Street in Manhattan was the South to us— brought back unpleasant memories for Mommy. She hates the South.

A few months after we arrived, a group of Delaware state troopers stopped a group of us on a dark highway one night after my older brother David, who was driving, made an illegal U-turn. The troopers were tall, arrogant, and unsympathetic. They surrounded the car full of black kids and white mother, shone flashlights everywhere, and made David, then a doctoral student at Columbia University, stand outside in the cold without his coat while they questioned him point-edly. They then hauled him into night court while the rest of us fol-lowed, frightened and angry. Mommy was furious that her shy, intellectual son—she was always so proud of David and would liter-ally have carried his books to school for him if he had asked her to—was placed before a judge, who asked him to announce whether he was "guilty" of the traffic infraction or not. She immediately jumped into F. Lee Bailey mode. "Don't say guilty!" she cried. "They'll lock you up!"

"Please, Ma," David said, trying to calm her as the judge looked on.

"No, no!" she shouted. "You're not guilty—*of nothing!*"

Looking back now, the whole incident was only a routine stop, ticket, and trip to night court, and when I later covered cops as a re-porter for the *Wilmington News Journal,* I saw a much better side of the Delaware state police. But Mommy did not have that insight, and from that moment on she hated Delaware. "We're *really* moving back to New York now," she said. "We haven't sold the house yet. We'll get out of that contract."

My sisters loaded the northbound Amtrak train at Wilmington, carrying their possessions in shopping bags. Contingency plans were made. Appointments were drawn up. Promises were struck: "Y'all fol-low us with the truck. . . . We'll enroll in school . . . talk to the princi-pal for me, okay? . . . See you in New York." And they were off.

Two hours later I talked Ma out of it. "What's back in New York?" I asked her. "There's nothing back there for us. It's over. You can't afford that house." Regretfully, she agreed. The girls called up from the city and she ordered them back home.

She was spinning in crazy circles only because she was trying to survive, and movement was always her *modus operandi* when things got tough. She was a fifty-four-year-old widow living off a small pension and social security with five kids still left to raise. She had never been on her own in terms of moving, checking out neighborhoods, buying houses, driving cars. It was a lot for anyone to do alone. Her job through two marriages—the first for sixteen years, the second for fourteen—had been to mother her children; but now she had to run a family, and she was learning late. She also was drained emotionally and felt tremendous guilt about moving us out of New York. She often sat at the kitchen table in the evening, brooding, "What have I done? What was I thinking?" staring off into space, holding a cup of cold, untouched coffee.

Prayer turned her around. That and the public school system, which forced her hand. When she saw the tattered books we brought home from school, she rose up like the Mommy of old. "You'll be a nothing, with this kind of education," she said. She bought an old, used Toyota for nine hundred dollars, took a driving course, and despite the fact that the driving instructor was a dirty old man who, in her words, "got fresh" with his hands, got her driver's license within two weeks. She opened up the phone book, ran her finger down the list of private and Catholic schools, called the schools, found out which ones had scholarships, and drove me up to one. The headmaster interviewed me for four hours. He gave me a writing test, a geography test, then laid a bunch of math on me which stumped me. If I hadn't missed so much school the previous two years, I might have smoked those tests, but I had barely passed the eleventh grade and was lucky to be a senior. The man wasn't sympathetic. He said because I'd be entering his school as a senior, I might not be able to adjust. The school turned me down.

I went to the all-black public Pierre S. Du Pont High School with my sisters Kathy and Judy and liked it fine. The kids called me "New York" like folks did in Louisville, but now I kept away from the hangout crowd and dealt with my music, focusing on tenor sax and trombone, which I picked up in order to play in the marching band. The change was good for me and I gave up weed and drinking for the discipline of music with the help of the school's outstanding music teacher, a black man named C. Lawler Rogers. Overall, the schoolwork in Delaware was ten times easier than the work in New York and I was selected to travel to Europe with the American Youth Jazz Band, which was organized by a very kind white music teacher from New Castle County named Hal Schiff.

The American Youth Jazz Band trip to Europe wasn't free. You had to pay for it, which I could not. My trip was paid for by a well-to-do couple from nearby Chadds Ford, Pennsylvania, named David H. and Ann Fox Dawson who had donated a good part of their lives and resources to inner city kids for many years. Mr. Dawson was a tall, trim gray-haired man who was senior vice president at the Du Pont company. He and his wife were the band's main sponsors, giving scholarships to needy musicians. In exchange, you had to work on their estate on weekends and during the summer, so in the space of a year I went from getting high on a street corner in Louisville to buttering parties for old-money blue bloods in cheeky Chadds Ford. I combed my Afro down, dressed in a suit and bow tie that Mrs. Dawson loaned me, and carried trays of hors d'oeuvres around—me and Pearl, the black woman who had done Mrs. Dawson's cooking and housework for years. Pearl lived in Wilmington like I did, and one day

I pulled her aside and asked her, "Why do you work for these white folks?" She looked at me like I was crazy. She and Mrs. Dawson were quite close. She said, "You out here too, ain't you?" and that shut me up. At the Dawson affairs, I quietly served chuckling white folks—the president of Du Pont and the governor of Delaware, among others. These people were nothing like me or my mother or anyone else in my family, but I had no anger toward them. My anger at the world had been replaced by burning ambition. I didn't want to be like them, standing around sipping wine and showing proper manners and acting happy when they weren't—I'm similar to my mother in that way—but these people had done nothing to me. I could see they were willing to help the band and indirectly me, because I was dying to go to Europe, so I was grateful to them. My expectations of them went no farther than that.

I was the clumsiest, worst party butler Mrs. Dawson ever had, and to her everlasting credit, she did not fire me right away. I wrinkled people's coats as I collected them, crushed their hats, spilled drinks, and dropped hors d'oeuvres everywhere. Mrs. Dawson was constantly saying, "James, carry the tray this way . . . no, *this* way . . . now put it over here. . . . Now straighten the tie . . . put the towel on the arm *like this*. . . . Hold the tray up, *up* . . . *oh my!*" *Crash!* Down went the tray. I liked Mrs. Dawson, despite the fact that I often made her cross. She was a demanding, witty, spry woman who was the first white person I ever had an ongoing dialogue with about music and literature, which she enjoyed greatly. She turned me on to classical composers and literary writers whom I had never heard of, tried to correct what she considered to be my poor speech and manners, which I did not like at all, and often made me sit with her and read poetry, the words of which later in life would suddenly pop into my memory out of nowhere, as if someone had planted them there, which she in fact had: *James James/Morrison Morrison/Weatherby George Dupree/Took great care of his Mother/Though he was only three. . . .*

Catering her parties wasn't my only job. I wasn't a total house Negro, so to speak. Most of my work was in the field. The estate was a huge piece of land, acres, encompassing a horse barn, a large vegetable garden, and a pool, tended by a young white caretaker named Harry. We cut grass, trimmed trees, cleaned the barn, ran a gerry tractor, and kept busy all day. Harry was a hillbilly and a smart dude who liked to hunt deer, and he kept a supply of beer and a long shotgun behind the seat of his pickup truck specifically for that purpose. I liked Harry and kept him laughing all day. He marveled at how I got out of doing all the dirty work Mrs. Dawson wanted me to do.

"James, you're a lazy guy," he told me one afternoon, "and if you don't tighten up, Mrs. D will find you out." I paid him no mind, but not long afterward his prophecy came true. I had to get up at five A.M. to catch a bus to Mrs. Dawson's from Wilmington and was often exhausted when I got there. One hot afternoon Mr. Dawson caught me sleeping in the strawberry patch that I was supposed to be weeding and told Mrs. Dawson about it. She got angry and fired me on the spot. "How can you fire me!" I said. "I've got to go to Europe!"

"I'm sending you to Europe," she said, "but you're fired anyway. You, *boy*, have to learn to work." Well, when she said I was going to Europe, I hugged her. I did mind her calling me boy but I didn't mind her firing me. She had done me a favor. I kept in touch with her for many years. She helped me through college and helped me get into graduate school as well; she didn't pay my way, but if I had an emergency, she would help. One morning a couple of years later when I was at Oberlin College, I went to my mailbox and found a letter from her telling me that her husband had died suddenly of cancer. Later that day I was standing on the street with a group of black students and one of them said, "Forget these whiteys. They're all rich. They got no problems," and I said, "Yeah, man, I hear you," while inside my pocket was the folded letter holding the heartbroken words of an old white lady who had always gone out of her way to help me—and many others like me. It hurt me a little bit to stand there and lie. Sometimes it seemed like the truth was a bandy-legged soul who dashed from one side of the world to the other and I could never find him.

By the time I began my senior year in high school, I knew I wanted to go to college and be a musician of some kind. I couldn't see myself hanging around Wilmington working at a 7-Eleven, gigging in a pop band that played the VFW and other seedy country joints, which is what I was doing. I did have an urge to stay out of school and study saxophone and jazz composition like the old-timers I admired—Bird, Coltrane, Clifford Brown—but I was afraid I might never get out of Delaware. Ma wanted me out of Delaware too, but she had no escape. She was the unhappiest I had ever seen her. It was like her legs were cut out from under her. The day before Thanksgiving in 1974, her old Toyota broke down and she had no money to fix it, which meant we had to take a bus to some godforsaken distant supermarket to find a turkey we could afford. We found the bird, but when we got on the bus to go home the paper bag holding the frozen turkey burst; it fell out of the bag and rolled all the way down the aisle to the front of the bus, where the driver grabbed it. The passengers and driver laughed, but to Ma this episode epitomized her entire experience in Delaware, that darned turkey rolling down the darned aisle in front of all those darned people. She had few friends there. The black folks found her to be awkward. The white folks bored her. But there was no quick and easy escape.

College was my way out. My eldest brother's wife, Becky, had gone to Oberlin College in Ohio and she told me I should apply because they had a great liberal arts school, a conservatory of music, and most of all, scholarship money. My high school grades were sour, my SATs low, but my musical and writing abilities were strong and I had good recommendations. To my utter amazement, the school accepted me. Mommy was completely happy when I told her the news. She hugged me and beamed, put the acceptance letter in her shoebox under her bed, and bragged to anyone she saw, in the supermarkets, at the library, "My son's going to Oberlin. You never heard of Oberlin? Oh, let me tell you . . ." I was the eighth straight child she sent to college. The seven before me all graduated and most went on for higher degrees.

On a cloudy, rainy day in September 1975, I packed everything I owned into an old green duffel bag and Ma drove me to the Greyhound bus station. As usual, she was broke, dumping single dollar bills, change, pennies on the counter to pay for the one-way ticket to Ohio. As I stepped on the bus she squeezed a bunch of bills and change into my hand. "It's all I have," she said. I counted it. Fourteen dollars. "Thanks, Ma." I kissed her and got on the bus quickly to hide my own tears. I felt I was abandoning her—she hated Delaware and I had talked her into staying there, and now I was leaving. Yet she wanted me to go. As I sat down on the bus and looked for her through the window, it occurred to me that since I was a little boy, she had always wanted me to go. She was always sending me off on a bus someplace, to elementary school, to camp, to relatives in Kentucky, to college. She pushed me away from her just as she'd pushed my elder siblings away when we lived in New York, literally shoving them out the front door when they left for college. She would not hear of it when they applied to schools that were near home. "If you stay here, you'll fool around," she'd say. "Go away and learn to live on your own." Yet she'd wipe her eyes with the back of her hand and watch silently through the living room window as they smiled and waved goodbye from the sidewalk, straining under the weight of the same cheap duffel bag that now lay in the belly of the Greyhound bus, holding my things. She always cried when they left, though never in front of us. She'd retreat to her room for that. I was actually worried she would cry when I boarded the bus, but when I looked at her through the window I was relieved to see she wasn't crying at all. She was pacing, puckering her lips, frowning, making faces. She paced this way and that, hands in her pockets, as the wind blew swirls of leaves and discarded paper cups about her feet. She was wearing a brown raincoat and a scarf over her head, a lone white woman marching back and forth on a dim street in front of the dilapidated bus station in Wilmington, Delaware, beneath a rumbling Amtrak train trestle and a cloudy sky. She seemed so agitated and jumpy I remember wondering if she had to go to the bathroom. As the bus engine rumbled to life, she didn't wave but rather gave a quick flip of the hand that said, "Go! Go on!" and hurried away. The bus pulled off and she was out of sight for a moment, but after we turned the corner I saw her from the window across the aisle and she had broken down. She was leaning on the wall beneath the train trestle, head bowed, one hand squeezing her eyes, as if the tears that flowed out of them could be squeezed into oblivion.

19.

The Promise

After my adventures with Rocky I was done with the fast life. I got a job at a diner
serving food to customers, and after a couple of weeks Dennis called on me again and
we started going out. He was a real serious man, thoughtful and solid, different from
Rocky and the other men I had seen in Harlem who hung around Small's Paradise.
Dennis was a violinist who had come to New York from High Point, North Carolina.
He came to New York in his middle twenties, which was a late age for most folks to
leave home in those days, but he was an only child and his mother, Etta, didn't want
him to leave home. She'd had a few miscarriages and Dennis was her only son, but he
went to New York because he wanted to pursue music. He played violin and read
music and composed it, mostly classical and religious music. Your father came from the
same town and went to the same high school as John Coltrane, but he was ahead of

Coltrane in age. Dennis used to sit around with stacks of sheet music when I first met him, scribbling at it and scoring it out. He played the violin beautifully and I'd often ask him to play various songs for me. He also was a good singer and sang in the Metropolitan Baptist Church choir in Harlem.

Dennis almost starved to death fooling around with that music, which is why I never wanted you fooling around with it when you decided to make a living at it. They wouldn't hire a black man for the orchestras or anything like that in those days and he scuffled around and slept in flophouses. What saved him were some friends from his hometown in High Point, Curtis and Minnie Ware. Curtis worked as a superintendent in an apartment house in Manhattan and he and Minnie were well-off compared to most black folks who came up from the South, because they lived rent-free. Curtis and Minnie housed and fed whole families that had migrated north from High Point, but Dennis was too proud to look them up. Only after he was starving and sleeping in flophouses did he tell them, "I've got no money and noplace to go," and they were angry with him. They said, "You should have come to us sooner." They had four other friends and a sister from the South, all crammed in their apartment. At mealtimes there was a huge round table, filled with all kinds of southern cooking, baked goods, and cold drinks. After Dennis got on his feet and got a job at my Aunt Mary's leather factory and we started going out, he brought me by there and said, "I want y'all to meet a friend of mine," and their eyes kind of popped out when I walked into the room.

This was around 1940 and black and white didn't do what me and Dennis were doing, walking around and such. Some folks did it, but it was all secret, or they were good-time, partying folks like Rocky's friends at Small's Paradise. But Dennis was a Christian man and a serious man and so were his friends. This was no joking matter to them.

Well, once they managed to pull their jaws from off the floor, they said, "Our house is your house. Sit down and eat." And I didn't have any problem with them, or with any of Dennis's family. They took me in with open hearts and made me one of their own; the only thing was it sometimes took a minute for them to get over the shock of seeing a black and white together—like Aunt Candis, Dennis's aunt. Aunt Candis was Dennis's favorite. She was the grandchild of slaves. When I first came to North Carolina and walked into her house, she said, "I just hope you excuse me for looking at you so hard, because I've never had a white person in my house before, and I've never been this close to a white person before." And I said, "All right," and she was my friend till she died. I'll never forget her as long as I live. She lived to be nearly a hundred. We wouldn't have made it without Aunt Candis. She came up from North Carolina and cared for y'all after Dennis died, because I was grieving and lost and I couldn't move. I couldn't move. She took the train all the way up to New York from North Carolina and took care of all eight of you, including you, James, and you weren't but a tiny child. She had never been to the city before. She'd never seen so much cement and so many tall buildings in her life. Your stepfather, he bought her a big gold watch after he married me and she left to go home to North Carolina. He said, "That's some woman," and he was right. She was some woman.

Well, Dennis was a solid, clean Christian man. He seemed to understand me and see right through me. It wasn't long before I fell in love with him and after a few months we started thinking of getting married. Well, I was thinking of getting married. Dennis hemmed and hawed on it and finally he said, "Let's live together as husband and wife. We don't need the world to know we're married. The world isn't ready for us yet." That excuse was okay for me—for the time being—so we rented a room in the Port Royal on 129th Street. We had a room in a three-bedroom apartment run by a lady named Mrs. Ellis. She and her husband had one bedroom and they rented the other two out and we shared the kitchen and bathroom.

Just like that I left home. I left Bubeh's apartment one day and never came back. See, Bubeh was old and she had diabetes and couldn't control me, and it wasn't like my aunts were calling to check on me or anything like that. They had their own lives and they didn't care about me. I was grown, child. I wasn't no baby then. "Get out there and do your own thing," that was their attitude. So I did my own thing. I moved in with Dennis and I didn't regret it. He continued to work for my Aunt Mary while I was living with him, and she never knew it.

It was a scandal, don't you think? But I did miss my mother. I missed her terribly and would think of her and my sister Dee-Dee often. One day I had a feeling, I just wanted to talk to Mameh, even though I knew she didn't agree with how I was living, so I got a pile of coins together and I went outside our little room on 129th Street to a pay phone and called Suffolk. Since Dennis and I lived in a room in some-body's apartment, to use the phone you had to sit in the woman's living room. I couldn't call my mother and talk Yiddish on the lady's phone. It seemed too odd to do. I was too embarrassed. So I went outside. It was a big deal to call long-distance in those days. When I called, Tateh picked up the line and he told me, "I don't know what you're doing up there, but your mother's sick and I need help with the store." So I came back to Suffolk. I didn't want to, but since Mameh was sick, I needed to go back. I told Dennis I was going home for a few weeks and he said he would write and send me money, which he did.

When I got to Virginia I told Tateh, "I'll help out for a while, but I'm not stay-ing." He ignored that. One of the first things he did was take me out to Portsmouth to one of his Jewish merchant friends, supposedly to "do business," and introduce me to this man's son. He was pressing me to marry this fat guy whom I didn't even know. But I had no plans on that. I'd come home for Mameh. She was getting more ill. [She had become nearly blind in her left eye and would black out.] She wasn't a total crip-ple, not even when she was ill was she truly crippled. She would cook all day and also darn socks. She could chop fish, meat, and vegetables on a butcher-block cutting board—all with one hand. She was a good Jewish wife who kept true to her religious faith, and she let a lot roll off her back over the years because her husband wasn't worth a dime and she had no choice. The way Tateh treated her, they'd call her an "abused woman" today. Back then they just called you "wife." And a man could do anything he wanted to his wife in the South. Especially if she's a Jew who's crippled and he's a so-called rabbi. He can yell at her, make fun of her, curse her, slap her. He can even go out with another woman right in front of her face.

She tried to ignore that, too, as long as she could, and I don't think she knew for a while because Tateh was always a little strange anyway, you know, and secretive. He never told us anything, like where he was born, or if he had any family or relatives.

Every summer he'd disappear for a few weeks to Europe. He'd say, "I'm going to see my landsman,*" and off he'd go on a steamer to France someplace. "Landsman" in Jewish is somebody from your hometown. We'd run the store in his absence, me, Dee-Dee, and Mameh. To this day I don't know exactly where he went, but a few weeks later he'd strut into the store, put down his bags, and say, "Where's my money?" We'd give it to him and he'd sit down and count it. Even before he took off his jacket, he'd count his money. He knew just how much he was supposed to earn a week, more or less. He was serious about his money.*

This big fat white lady started showing up at the store around 1939 or 1940. She had a behind as big as this living room. She lived not far from us up the road. Her husband was serving time in the county jail across the street for being drunk or some petty crime like that. She wasn't Jewish and she had four or five kids. Tateh would talk to her in the store and try to act like it was casual; then on Friday nights, the Sabbath, Mr. Rabbi would go out. Me, Dee-Dee, and Mameh would light the candles and say our prayers to begin the Sabbath, and Tateh would pack a bag of groceries and throw them in his car while Mameh watched him. He'd say to her in Yiddish, "I'm going out." Then he'd say to me in English, "I won't be back till Monday. Open up the store Sunday morning."

Then Mameh would ask me, "What did he say?"

"Nothing," I'd say.

Their marriage was falling apart and I was in the middle. I'd translate, or not translate, between them. Tateh's affair became full-blown very quickly, the way I remember it. Before I knew it he'd moved her and her kids across the North Carolina line someplace about an hour's drive from Suffolk, and he once even dragged me down there and made me wait outside the woman's house while he ran inside. He started bothering me to get Mameh to give him a divorce, trying to talk to her through me. She refused, and I could understand her dilemma. She was in her early forties then, and there was nobody to look out for her. She was handicapped. She was sick. She had no other home. She was not giving him a divorce. Never. I don't think she had one friend down in Suffolk at that time either, not that I remember. Except for her mother she had nobody to turn to, because her sisters never cared for her that much. She was just a crippled thing to them, and they rarely wrote to her and never gave her any credit for the good things she had done. Their way of being kind to her was to take me in during the summers and by then they were done with me because I wasn't a child anymore. And here Tateh wanted to divorce her so he could marry his fat girlfriend, this woman who was bigger and taller than him and who wasn't even Jewish. A goye. It was all so disgusting I could hardly stand it.

In order for my parents to get a divorce properly in the Jewish faith they would've had to go to a rov, a kind of high Jewish rabbi, but Tateh didn't care for no rov. He was done with being religious. He went out to a lawyer one day and came back with some papers and laid them on the table and told me, "Tell your mother to sign these." They were divorce papers. Mameh refused. Then he went to Reno, Nevada, and got himself a quickie divorce. He came back to Virginia and said, "Tell your mother we're divorced," and that was it. But nothing changed in my house. We all still lived together, and we were all miserable, and by this time I was home a few weeks, a lot longer than I had planned, and I wanted to leave. It was a miserable time, especially for my poor sister Dee-Dee. Dee-Dee was four years younger than me, only about fifteen then. What a life she'd had. Of all of us children, Dee-Dee had the worst of it, because she was the youngest.

Dee-Dee didn't seem to have problems. I always thought she was prettier than me. She wasn't rebellious like I was. We were like night and day. She was short and had curly brown hair while I was tall and dark and thin and had a mustache. When she was little she refused to wear hand-me-downs and wore nice skirts and socks and always looked neat, whereas I would wear hand-me-downs and looked like a sack of potatoes no matter what I wore. Dee-Dee was very smart. She got good grades in school while me and my brother Sam barely passed. She was Tateh's favorite and I was always a little jealous of her because Tateh paid for her piano lessons while he wouldn't allow me to take them and that sort of thing. See, she was the first American in my family, while Sam and I were immigrants, and we kind of had that immigrant thing on us. The kids would make fun of us for being Jewish in school, but they wouldn't make fun of Dee-Dee. You just didn't do that to Dee-Dee. She had confidence. She was a nice Jewish girl who did what she was told. I mean, she was in high school going through the things high school girls go through, playing tennis and learning piano, and when Tateh was divorcing Mameh she got lost in all that. No one ever talked to her or shared feelings with her, including me. We were close—not close enough for me to tell her the mess I had made of my life, but close enough—and one evening she came up to our bedroom and said, "I know you're going to leave, Rachel. Don't leave. Don't go back to New York." Dee-Dee was so proud, and for her to ask me to stay . . . well, she meant it. We didn't talk to each other that way, and for her to come out and say what she was feeling was hard for her. It hurt me so much to hear it because I couldn't stay. "I'll think about it," I said.

"I don't believe you," she said. "I know you're going back. Please don't go back. Promise me you'll stay." She sat on the bed and buried her face in her hands and cried, my little sister. "Promise me," she sobbed. "Promise me you'll stay."

"Okay, I promise," I said. "I'll stay." But I broke my promise to Dee-Dee and she never forgot it. And she would remind me of it many years later.

20.

Old Man Shilsky

It was November 1982, and I was tooling down Virginia State Route 460 in my green 1972 Volkswagen at four A.M. A few hours before, I had dropped off my ex-girlfriend, Karen, a black model who renamed herself Karone ("My agent told me to do it") at her grandmother's house in Petersburg. Also in tow with her was her two-year-old son, Paul, a gentle, kind boy who seemed slightly confused as to who I was. Mommy hated Karone. "You got a ready-made family now," she quipped. "Your whole life was in front of you. Now look at you."

"What do you mean?" I asked.

"Bye-bye dreams!" she sniffed.

I ignored her. Karone and I had no plans to get married. We were not close. We were both living in Boston and decided it was time to leave town as well as each other. She was leaving her ex-husband behind. I wanted to leave myself behind. I had been working as a feature writer at the *Boston Globe,* a great job for a twenty-four-year-old reporter. My best friend was a white guy about sixty years old named Ernie Santosuosso who was the *Globe* jazz critic then. We would walk around the features department singing "Polka Dots and Moonbeams" and "It's You or No One" by saxophonist Dexter Gordon. I could've stayed there with Ernie forever, dogging it and cracking jokes in the features department, but I couldn't decide whether I wanted to be a writer or a musician, not knowing that it was possible to do both. In some ways I was caught between the worlds of black and white as well, because I'd discovered after college and graduate school that the earnest change-the-world rap sessions me and my schoolmates had that lasted till four A.M. didn't change the world one iota. I can clearly remember saying to my black college roommate in my freshman year, "Racism is a problem that should end just about the time we graduate." Instead it smashed me across the face like a bottle when I walked into the real world. Boston was not an easy place to have a racial identity crisis either. Its racial problems are complicated, spilling over into matters of class, history, politics, even education. It was more than I wanted to face, and I had to run.

On the seat next to me was a small map of Virginia with the town of Suffolk circled on it, and a hand-drawn map Mommy had given me. It had taken years to solicit this information about where she grew up. Every time I'd ask about it, she'd say, "Oh yeah, well, there's nobody there that remembers me," and off she went, looking for a house, or chasing down some errand that lasted hours, days, or weeks. It had gotten to the point where I didn't see why she made such a secret of it, and the part of me that wanted to understand who I was began to irk and itch at me, like a pesky mosquito bite that cries out to be scratched. When I finally nailed her down on it, she sat at the kitchen table, pulled out an old envelope, ripped it open, and unfolded it to give her more space. She then drew me a map of where she had lived in Suffolk. She talked as she drew: "The highway goes here. Here's the bridge. The courthouse is down the road, and the Jaffe slaughterhouse is over here. . . ." That map was the only clue I had to lead me to Mommy's family. She knew no names of people in Suffolk, despite having lived there for nearly thirteen years. "You can't remember anybody?" I asked.

"Nope."

"Nobody?"

"Well, I knew a girl named Frances."

"Who was she?"

"She was my best friend."

"Where is she now?"

"God knows."

"What about her family."

"Don't remember them. But her mother could cook like the dickens."

So I went to Suffolk looking for Frances and her mother who could cook like the dickens. Mommy didn't remember their last name.

It was seven A.M. when I arrived in town, exhausted and hungry after the drive from Petersburg. The town looked like its sugar days were over. Quiet, empty, a mix of grand old buildings and new, more of an industrial site than a town really, with development sprawling into its surrounding areas rather than inside the town itself. I saw a McDonald's at a corner intersection. I parked there, went inside, and ordered some food. I sat down at a table and opened Mommy's little hand map. I checked the map, looked out the window, checked it again, looked out the window again. I knew I was on Main Street. There was an old courthouse building catty-corner to where I sat. Behind the courthouse was a graveyard. To my left was a bridge and a slaughterhouse. I was sitting right where her family's store used to be, 601 North Main Street. I left the food untouched and went outside and looked around. There was an old house behind the McDonald's. I knocked on the door and an elderly, bespectacled black man answered. I told him my business: Mother used to live here. Name was Shilsky. Jews. A little store. He fingered his glasses and stared at me a long time. Then he said, "C'mon in here."

He sat me down and brought me a soda. Then he asked me to tell my story one more time. So I did.

He nodded and listened closely. Then his face broke into a smile. "That means you ol' Rabbi Shilsky's grandson?"

"Yep."

First he chuckled. Then he laughed. Then he laughed some more. He tried to control his laughing but he couldn't, so he stopped, took off his glasses, and wiped his eyes. I started to get angry, and he apologized. His name was Eddie Thompson. He was sixty-six. He had lived in that house all his life. It took him a minute to get himself together.

"I knew your mother," he said. "We used to call her Rachel."

I had never heard that name before. Even in recounting what little she had told me of her life, Mommy had never referred to herself as Rachel. She had always called herself Ruth. I discovered later that her true name was Ruchel, a Yiddish name which her family Americanized to Rachel, which she in turn further changed to the even more American-sounding Ruth.

"I knew that whole family," Thompson said. "Rachel, Gladys, Sam, and the parents. Rachel was the kindhearted one. Gladys, the young one, we called her Dee-Dee. She was a li'l bitty thing. She looked more like the father. Sam, the brother, we used to call him Sparky. They say he got killed in World War Two in a plane crash. Rachel, why she used to walk right up and down the road here, her and the mother. The mother was crippled. She used to limp. Her whole left side was messed up, Mrs. Shilsky. What a nice lady. She'd slip you a piece of fruit or candy inside the store when the old man wasn't looking. Old Man Shilsky though . . ." He shrugged. "Personally, I never had no problem with him."

"What was he like?" I asked, my heart pounding. *Why is my heart pounding?* I asked myself. I wasn't sure.

"Like?" he asked.

"Old Man Shil—My grandfa—" I didn't know what to call him. Neither one sounded right. "What was Shilsky like?" I asked.

"Well . . . you being his grandson and all . . ." He shrugged again. "He . . . The old man was all right. I got along with him okay."

I could see in his face that he didn't believe it, so I said, "You don't have to spare me. I never knew him. I'd just like to know what he was like."

He cut a quick glance at the window, then said evenly, "You won't find anyone around here who liked him enough to even talk about him."

"Why so?"

"His dislike for the colored man was very great."

"How so?"

"Well . . . he just disliked black folks. And he cheated them. Sold 'em anything and everything and charged 'em as much as he could. If you owed him five dollars he'd make you pay back ten. He shot ol' Lijah Ricks in the stomach. Lijah brought that on himself though, went in the Shilskys' store fussin' over some sardines and crackers and wouldn't pay. Shilsky shot him in the left or right side, I can't remember which. He didn't kill him, but he was a hateful one, Old Man Shilsky. His own wife was scared of him."

"How do you know all this?"

"Know? Why I could practically see into the man's house from my bedroom. We were right next door. I worked for Shilsky at one time. Made ten cents a day firing up his stove on Saturday mornings 'cause Jews can't do much on Saturday. That's their Sunday, you see. He had a kerosene stove that left black marks everywhere. I wonder what happened to it. . . ." He pondered it a minute before I brought him back to the subject at hand. "He had a good thing there," Eddie Thompson said, "making money hand over fist off the Negro. But see, he was mean as a dog. Mrs. Shilsky was terrified of the old man. If she was talking to you and he came into the room, she'd shush up and tremble."

I listened in silence, his words landing on me like bricks. "What happened to him?" I asked.

"He run off with one of the sorriest, trashiest, poor-as-Job's-turkey white women you ever did see. I don't know how he got mixed up with her. She was a Claxton, Richard Claxton's wife. The old man, he fell in love with her because of Mrs. Shilsky being like she was, I reckon. That woman was big as a house. He looked like a boy when he walked down the road next to her. He was a little bitty guy." He laughed, bittersweet. "Ol' Man Shilsky. Boy, he was something else."

"You have any idea where he went?"

"Nope. Maybe Richmond. Don't know for sure."

"I'd sure like to find him," I said.

"Oh, I know where you can find him," the old black man said. He pointed down to the ground and winked. "They'd let him in down there even if the bridge was out. They'd parachute him over."

He talked for a long time, chuckling, disbelieving. "Rachel just left one day. I'm telling you she left, and we thought she was dead. That whole family is long gone. We didn't think we'd ever see none of them again till we got to the Other Side. And now you pop up. Lord knows it's a great day."

He asked if he could call Mommy. I picked up the phone and dialed Mommy's house long-distance, got her on the phone, and told her I had somebody who wanted to talk to her. I handed the phone to him.

"Rachel? Yeah. Rachel. This is Eddie Thompson. From down in Suffolk. Remember me? We used to live right be—Yeaaaaaah, that's right." Pause. "Naw. Everybody's dead now but Molly, Helen, Margaret, and Edward. That's right . . . Well, I'll be! The Lord touched me today!"

He paused a moment, listening.

"Rachel? That ain't you crying now, is it? This is old Eddie Thompson. You remember me? Don't cry now. . . ."

21.

A Bird Who Flies

In the summer of 1941, before I came back to New York to stay with Dennis in Harlem, we received a letter in Suffolk from Mameh's family in New York. It said, "We have three rooms' worth of furniture. Do you want it?" Bubeh lived in a three-room apartment. That's how they told us Bubeh was dead. They didn't even bother to write to Mameh, but rather wrote to Tateh in English, which Mameh didn't read nor understand. Tateh read the letter and tossed it to me. "Read this to your mother," he said, and walked away.

I waited till evening to read it to her, which meant she was walking around the store all day not knowing her mother was dead, and Tateh knew it, and I knew it, and it was just a mess. I read it to her in her bedroom, the one she shared with me and Dee-Dee. She had a little rocking chair that she sat in, and she was sitting there, looking out the window, when I came into the room. I said, "Mameh, I have something to read to you," and I read it to her. She never said a word. She just sat there and stared into the night, tears rolling down her face. Not a sound came from her lips. Not a word.

Later on, I went to bed and I heard a little noise coming from her bed. She slept in a little bed, by herself. I heard this little noise coming from her bed, and I knew she was crying and I said, "It's all right, Mameh, it's all right," but she just cried and cried. Just weeping. I can still hear her weeping now sometimes. I know the exact sound of it, like a note you hear or a song that keeps spinning around in your head and you can't forget it. Every once in a while when I'm walking down the street I think I hear it, just a quick sniffle noise, like an "oh!" and I turn around and no one's there.

I stuck around Suffolk awhile longer, and then I left for good sometime in 1941. I can't remember the exact time of all this because it was a bad time. It was bad. I left over Mameh's objections too. She said, "You can have a good life here," but I said, "I can't live here, Mameh," and she didn't bring it up ever again or ask me to stay any longer. There was no life in Suffolk for me. I packed what few things I wanted and tried to talk to Dee-Dee before I left, but she wouldn't talk to me. "You promised you wouldn't go," she said, and she walked away from me. As I left the store to walk downtown to the bus station, Mameh handed me a bag lunch and kissed me and I was out the door and gone. I never saw her or Dee-Dee ever again. Tateh didn't say a word to me as I walked out.

The Greyhound bus station was across from the Suffolk Hotel in those days. I was standing there waiting for the bus to come, when Tateh pulled up in his car. He kept a big V-8 Ford. He got out and took his hands out of his pockets and started pacing. He said, "You should stay."

I said, "I can't." I was nervous. He always made me nervous.

"I'll get you a route," he said. "You can have your own route, selling supplies to farmers in the country. You'll make a bundle. Or you can get a job in Norfolk. You can move there."

I said no.

"You want to go to college? I'll send you to college in Norfolk. Or business school, whatever you want, but you have to stay."

"I can't do that."

"I'm telling you to stay," he said. "Hear me? I need you to run the store. And your mother needs you."

I began to yell at him and we argued. Here he was having divorced Mameh and he was still using her against me. Then he said, "I know you're gonna marry a shvartse. *You're making a mistake." That stopped me cold, because I didn't know how he learned it. To this day I don't know. He said, "If you marry a nigger, don't ever come home again. Don't come back."*

"I'll always come to see Mameh."

"Not if you marry a nigger you won't," he said. "Don't come back."

He got in his car and left. When the bus came I got on it and cried a little and then fell asleep. When I woke later on, I opened the lunch bag Mameh had packed for me and inside, tucked between the knishes and matzoh balls and chopped liver, was her Polish passport, with her picture inside. It's the only picture I have of her, she's sitting down holding me and my brother Sam in her lap.

A few weeks after I got back to New York and was living with Dennis in Harlem, Dennis overheard my Aunt Mary say that Tateh had put out a detective to look for me. It just made me lay low in Harlem. I was never going back home. Instead I got a job at a glass factory down in the Chelsea area of Manhattan. My job was to hold these glass tubes over fire and stretch them into test tubes. I would come home from work every night with big burns on my hands. Not long after, in early '42, Dennis came home from Aunt Mary's factory and told me he heard Aunt Mary say that my mother was sick and had been brought up to a hospital in the Bronx. I right away went out and called Aunt Mary and asked if she knew where Mameh was. She said, "You're out of the family. Stay out. We sat shiva for you. You can't see her." Well, that just hurt me to the bone. That night I told Dennis, "I've got to see her." He said,

"Ruth, your Aunt Mary made it clear that you're not welcome up there." That gave me pause. I didn't want to make Mameh sicker. After all, I was out of the family. I worried sick about it, trying to think what to do and I could not decide.

A few days later I was at work at the glass factory and the foreman, a German man, came over to me and told me I had a phone call. It was Dennis. He was calling from Aunt Mary's factory. He told me Mameh had just passed away.

They had a locker room in the glass factory where we changed and put on our work aprons, and I hung up the phone and went in there and howled out my grief. The foreman and other workers came in there and tried to help me stand because I had fallen to the floor, but I couldn't get up. I tried to, but I couldn't, and one of the ladies was saying, "Oh, she don't have to act like that, hollering and carrying on."

I was depressed for months. I lost weight and couldn't eat and was near suicide. I kept saying, "Why couldn't it have been me that died?" I would go on long walks and would forget where I was. I'd be someplace and couldn't remember how I got there. Dennis was the one who shook me out of it. He kept saying. "You've got to forgive yourself, Ruth. God forgives you. He'll forgive the most dreaded sin, the most dreaded sin." But I couldn't listen, not for a long while, I couldn't listen. I was so so sorry, deep in my heart I was sorry, but all your "sorrys" are gone when a person dies. She was gone. Gone. That's why you have to say all your "sorrys" and "I love yous" while a person is living, because tomorrow isn't promised. Lord, I was burning with hurt. I hung on to Mameh's passport and carried it everywhere. I didn't think she was dying when I left home, but she knew it. That's why she gave me that passport. I've always held that to this day, that guilt, that I left Mameh, because all her life I was the one who translated for her and helped her around. I was her eyes and ears in America, and when I left . . . well, Sam had gone, and Bubeh had died, and her husband treated her so bad and divorced her, and her reasons for living just slipped away. It was a bad time.

It took a long time to get over it, but Dennis stuck it out with me, and after a while I began to listen to what he said about God forgiving you, and I began to hold on to that, that God will forgive you, will forgive the most dreaded sin, because I felt

Mameh deserved better from me, and that's when I started going to Metropolitan Church in Harlem with Dennis to hear Rev. Brown preach. It helped me to hear the Christian way, because I needed help, I needed to let Mameh go, and that's when I started to become a Christian and the Jew in me began to die. The Jew in me was dying anyway, but it truly died when my mother died.

I remember how she used to laugh when she waved chickens over our heads on Yom Kippur. I bet they don't even do that now. She'd wave a live chicken over her head and say to the chicken, "You to death, me to life!" while we'd scream and run away because my father would take the chicken from her and kill it as a blood sacrifice. I didn't like that. It seemed so old-fashioned and odd. "I don't want to do that in America," I'd say. But she'd say, "That chicken is just showing God we're thankful for living. It's just a chicken. It's not a bird who flies. A bird who flies is special. You would never trap a bird who flies." She used to sit in a little rocking chair in her room upstairs and watch the birds. She'd lay crumbs on the ledge of her window and the birds would gather there and eat while she sang to them, but she'd always shoo them away and make them fly off so they'd be free again. She had a little Yiddish song she used to sing to them. "Feygele, feygele, gay a veck." *"Birdie, birdie, fly away."*

22.

A Jew Discovered

It was afternoon, August 1992, and I was standing in front of the only synagogue in downtown Suffolk, a collection of old storefronts, dimly lit buildings, and old railroad tracks that tell of better, more populous times. It's a small, old, white building with four tall columns and a row of stairs leading to a tall doorway. This is the synagogue that young Rachel Shilsky walked to with her family and where Rabbi Shilsky led the congregation during the Jewish holidays Rosh Hashana, the Jewish New Year, and Yom Kippur, the day of atonement and fasting. When I was a boy, Jewish holidays meant a day off from school for me and that was it. I certainly had no idea they had anything to do with me.

I felt like an oddball standing in front of the quiet, empty building, and looked up and down the street every couple of minutes lest
the cops come by and wonder why a black man was loitering in front
of a white man's building in the middle of the day in Suffolk, Virginia. This is, after all, the nineties, and any black man who loiters in
front of a building for a long time looking it over is bound to draw
suspicion from cops and others who probably think he's looking for
an open entrance so he can climb in and steal something. Black males
are closely associated with crime in America, not with white Jewish
mothers, and I could not imagine a police officer buying my story as I
stood in front of the Jewish temple saying, "Uh, yeah, my grandfather
was the rabbi here, you know . . ." The sun was baking the sidewalk
and it was so hot I sat down on the steps, placing my tape recorder
and notebook next to me.

My long search for the Shilsky family ended here. I had spent con-
siderable time looking through school records, court records, and
other documents with mixed results. My grandmother Hudis was
buried far from here, in a Long Island graveyard amongst hundreds
and hundreds of Jews, more than she ever had the pleasure of living
around down here. The U.S. Army forked over the death record of
Sergeant Sam Shilsky, who died in February 1944, but the details of
his service record were gone forever, lost in a fire of army personnel
records. I felt like I was stalking ghosts. No sign of Rabbi Shilsky,
whom I traced to a Brooklyn address in the 1960s, where he appar-
ently landed after wandering through Norfolk, Virginia; Belleville,
New Jersey; and Manhattan. Dee-Dee vanished from Suffolk shortly
before her mother died, and never returned. She withdrew from Suffolk High on January 23, 1942, one semester short of graduation.
Her mother died five days later, on January 28, 1942, in New York
City. I could only imagine how painful that must have been, having to

leave the only real home she ever had at age seventeen, her mother gone, her father with a gentile woman, her brother in the war, her sister disappeared; being completely helpless as the pillars of her life fell away like toothpicks. Everything she had known was gone. Whom did she live with? Maybe the father kept her. Who knows? I had a feeling she was still alive. She would have been about sixty-seven then. I could have tracked her down—I was, after all, a reporter—but after a couple of feeble attempts I gave up. I didn't have the heart. I didn't want to introduce any more pain into her life. She'd seen enough. The closest I could come to her was to sit on these synagogue steps, baking in the August heat, and wonder.

I wanted to see the inside of the synagogue. I wanted to see it, then later tell my black wife and my two children about it—because some of my blood runs through there, because my family has a history there, because there's a part of me in there whether I, or those that run the synagogue, like it or not. In truth, I had never been inside an actual synagogue before, the closest being the time I was working as a reporter and did a story about a Jewish school in Queens that had a synagogue attached to it. In the course of interviewing the headmaster, a woman, I mentioned that my mother was Jewish and she exclaimed, "Well, according to Jewish law that means you're Jewish too! We have a black Jew who works in our school!" She hit the intercom button on her desk phone and said, "Sam, can you come up here a minute?" Minutes later the black janitor walked in, holding a mop, smiling. I'd pay good money for a picture of my face at that moment. Ol' Sam smiled and said hello and I gurgled out a polite response, though I wanted to choke myself for opening up my big mouth.

When I called the rabbi of my mother's old synagogue he spoke to me with neither nostalgia nor surprise, only grudging recognition. He had heard I was in town from other Jews whom I had met. He knew I was black and he knew who my mother was. "I remember your mother," he said. I explained to him that I was writing a book about my family and asked if I might see some of the synagogue records. "There's nothing in them that would help you," he said curtly. I asked if I could see the inside of the synagogue itself. He said, "I'll have to check with some other board members to see who would have time to open it up to let you see it," and hung up. I knew the deal. Given the photo of the board members on the synagogue's anniversary pamphlet I'd obtained, I doubted if half the old geezers on the board were still drawing air. I hung up, muttering to myself, "I didn't want to see your silly old synagogue anyway."

By then I had seen enough anyway. The smell of azaleas and the creeping loneliness that climbed over me as I poked around Suffolk had begun to suffocate me. The isolation my family had felt, the heartbreak they had suffered, seemed to ooze out of the trees, curling through the stately old brick buildings and rising like steam off the Civil War statue that seemed to point its cannon directly at me as I wandered through the town graveyard. I wanted to leave right at that moment, but instead sat on the synagogue steps as if glued, as my mind reeled back to a previous trip in 1982, when fate and luck led me deep into the bowels of a state office building where Aubrey Rubenstein was working for the highway department right-of-way office. Rubenstein was in his early sixties then, a heavyset man with dark hair, a deep southern accent, and a very clear and concise manner. His father had taken over my grandfather's store around 1942 after the old man left town. When I walked into his office and explained who I was, he looked at me a long, long time. He didn't smile. He didn't frown. Finally he spoke: "What a surprise," he said softly. He offered me a seat and a cup of coffee. I accepted. "Don't move from there," he said.

He got on the phone. "Jaffe," he said, "I have incredible news. Fishel Shilksy's grandson is here. Sitting in my office. No kidding. . . . Uh-huh. And you won't believe it. He's black. No. I'm not lying. He's a reporter writing a book about his family. . . . Yep." When he hung up the phone, he said, "When we're done, go around to the slaughter-house on Main and see Gerry Jaffe and his family. They'd like to see you in person." I knew the name Jaffe. Mommy had spoken of them several times. *The Jaffes had a slaughterhouse down the road. Tateh would take us there to slaughter the cows in the kosher faith.* . . . I made it a point to go see them. Like most of the Jews in Suffolk they treated me very kindly, truly warm and welcoming, as if I were one of them, which in an odd way I suppose I was. I found it odd and amazing when white people treated me that way, as if there were no barriers between us. It said a lot about this religion—Judaism—that some of its followers, old southern crackers who talked with southern twangs and wore straw hats, seemed to believe that its covenants went beyond the color of one's skin. The Sheffers, Helen Weintraub, the Jaffes, they talked to me in person and by letter in a manner and tone that, in essence, said "Don't forget us. We have survived here. Your mother was part of this. . . ."

Sitting in his office, Aubrey Rubenstein talked easily, as a black colleague sat nearby eavesdropping with awe at the macabre conversation that unfolded between this elderly white man and myself. "There are not that many of us left," Aburey said. "We had maybe twenty-five or thirty Jewish families here at one time, back when your grandfather was around. The older ones died, the younger ones left. Some went to California, some to Virginia Beach, or just moved. The only ones who stayed had businesses with their fathers that dropped down to them."

"Why did they all leave?" I asked.

"Why stay?" he said. "It was not that easy a place for a Jew to live.

It was a tiny population of Jews. Most were merchants of one type or another. I suppose some found it easier to make a living elsewhere." Wandering Jews, I thought.

We spoke easily for quite a while. "It's an interesting thing that you've come down to check on your granddaddy," he said. "It's quite a story, I must say."

I asked him about my family. "Well, it was kind of a tragedy, really. Shilsky wasn't the man he could have been. He was a good rabbi—by that I mean he knew what he was teaching. In fact, he taught me a little as a boy. But he went into business full-time, which didn't please a lot of Jews here, and he was seeing another woman for years. I'm not sure whether he was divorced when he left here or not, but I ran into him in New York after the war, maybe '46. Me and another fella went to see him about buying the piece of property next door to his store. He was up in Brooklyn."

"What was he doing there?"

"I don't know. But I believe Mrs. Shilsky had died by then. The whole thing was very tragic." Seeing the expression on my face, he added, "Your grandmother was a fine lady. I still remember her coming to temple, lighting the candles, and standing up to say her prayers. I remember her clearly. She was crippled in the leg. She was a very fine lady."

I asked him if anyone knew how Rabbi Shilsky treated his family, and Rubenstein shrugged.

"There are things that you hear, but no one asked. He was tight with his money and they could have been doing better than they looked. The Shilskys kept to themselves. Your Uncle Sam, he joined the air force and got killed in a plane crash in Alaska. They didn't find his body or that of the other pilot for a long time, if they ever did find them. I heard this and don't know it to be true or not. Your Aunt

Gladys, you don't know her, do you? She was a very bright girl. Your mother . . . well, she was a fine girl. Of course we had heard rumors, and I'm being frank, that she had run off and married a black man, but I never knew it to be true or not. My daddy at one time said it, but my parents never gave it any further comment. My father and mother were like liberals in their days. I never heard them knock anybody for being white or black or green or Christian or Jew or Catholic."

I said nothing, listening in silence. I imagined that the news of Mommy's marriage crashed through the Jewish community like an earthquake.

"How is your mother?" he asked.

"Fine."

"You know," he said, fingering the papers on his desk, "you look a little bit like your mother. The smile. Do you attend temple, being part Jewish?"

"No. She didn't raise us Jewish."

"Well, maybe that was for the best," he said.

I was surprised by his candidness and said so.

We talked for a while longer before I rose to go. "Next time you come back I'll see if I can dig up a picture of that old store," he said. "Make sure to tell your mother Aubrey Rubenstein said hello."

I pointed to my tape player on his desk. "The tape is running," I said. "You can say it yourself."

He leaned over to the tape and spoke into it softly. When he was done, he leaned back in his chair, and looked at the ceiling thoughtfully. "She picked that life for herself and she lived it, that's all. What her reasons for it were I don't know. But she did a good job. She raised twelve children. She led a good life."

I told him I'd be back in a few months. "I'll have a picture of that store for you," he promised. But I waited ten years to come back, and when I called on him again he had died. I kept the tape with his greeting to Mommy on it for years, and while I never played it for her, thinking it might be too emotional for her to hear it, I played it for myself many times, thinking, wishing, hoping that the world would be this open-minded, knowing that God is: *Ruth, this is Aubrey Rubenstein. I don't know if you remember me or not, but if you do, I'm glad to meet your son and I see you've accomplished a great deal in your life. If you're ever down this way stop on by and say hello to us. We all remember you. We wish you the best.*

As I sat on the steps of the synagogue in the hot August sun, his words sliced through my memory like raindrops. I watched as two little black girls strode by, waved, and walked on. One was eating a bag of potato chips. I said to myself, "Whatever I'm looking for, I've found it." I got in my car and drove back to the McDonald's where the store had been. I walked around the grounds once again, as if the earth would speak to me. But it did not. It was just a cement parking lot. They ought to take the whole kit and caboodle of these cement parking lots and heave them into the sea, I thought. The Shilskys were gone. Long gone.

That night I slept in a motel just down the road from the McDonald's, and at about four in the morning I sat straight up. Something just drew me awake. I tossed and turned for an hour, then got dressed and went outside, walking down the road toward the nearby wharf. As I walked along the wharf and looked over the Nansemond River, which was colored an odd purple by the light of the moon, I said to myself, "What am I doing here? This place is so lonely. I gotta get out of here." It suddenly occurred to me that my grandmother had walked around here and gazed upon this water many times, and the loneliness and agony that Hudis Shilsky felt as a Jew in this lonely southern town—far from her mother and sisters in

New York, unable to speak English, a disabled Polish immigrant whose husband had no love for her and whose dreams of seeing her children grow up in America vanished as her life drained out of her at the age of forty-six—suddenly rose up in my blood and washed over me in waves. A penetrating loneliness covered me, lay on me so heavily I had to sit down and cover my face. I had no tears to shed. They were done long ago, but a new pain and a new awareness were born inside me. The uncertainty that lived inside me began to dissipate; the ache that the little boy who stared in the mirror felt was gone. My own humanity was awakened, rising up to greet me with a handshake as I watched the first glimmers of sunlight peek over the horizon. There's such a big difference between being dead and alive, I told myself, and the greatest gift that anyone can give anyone else is life. And the greatest sin a person can do to another is to take away that life. Next to that, all the rules and religions in the world are secondary; mere words and beliefs that people choose to believe and kill and hate by. My life won't be lived that way, and neither, I hope, will my children's. I left for New York happy in the knowledge that my grandmother had not suffered and died for nothing.

23.

Dennis

In 1942 Dennis and I were living in a room in the Port Royal on 129th Street between Seventh and Eighth Avenues, and one night after work I walked into the hallway of our building and this black woman punched me right in the face. She hit me so hard I fell to the floor. "Don't disrespect me!" she said. She was a raving lunatic. I never even knew who she was. I somehow got off the floor and she chased me up to our room and I slammed the door on her and waited for my husband to get home. Dennis went to speak to her when he got home from work. "That white woman don't belong here," she said. That's what she told him. Dennis didn't attack her. He just said, "Leave my wife alone," and she did. Even though we were not married, we considered ourselves husband and wife.

Some black folks never did accept me. Most did, but there were always a few running around saying "Nubian this" and "Nubian that" and always talking about Africa and all this. Well, I'm a mother of black children, and nobody will ever deny me my children, and they can put that in their Nubian pipe and smoke it. All this Nubian. If you want to go back to Africa, James, well, you can go. I don't see the point in your going when you have your family here. But if you feel you want to go to Africa to find your roots I won't stop you. I'll still be your mother when you come back. And you'll still be my son.

There was no turning back after my mother died. I stayed on the black side because that was the only place I could stay. The few problems I had with black folks were nothing compared to the grief white folks dished out. With whites it was no question. You weren't accepted to be with a black man and that was that. They'd say forget it. Are you crazy? A nigger and you? No way. They called you white trash. That's what they called me. Nowadays these mixed couples get on TV every other day complaining, "Oh, it's hard for us." They have cars and televisions and homes and they're complaining. Jungle fever they call it, flapping their jaws and making the whole thing sound stupid. They didn't have to run for their lives like we did. Me and Dennis caused a riot on 105th Street once. A bunch of white men chased us up the street and surrounded Dennis and tried to kill him, throwing bottles and hitting and kicking him until one of them made the rest of them stop. He said, "Get out of here while you can!" and we ran for it. See, most interracial marriages did not last. That's what Dennis would say when we argued. I'd say, "I'm leaving," and he'd say, "Go ahead. Go ahead. That's what people want us to do. That's what they expect." And he was right.

See, a marriage needs love. And God. And a little money. That's all. The rest you can deal with. It's not about black or white. It's about God and don't let anyone tell you different. All this Jungle fever! Shoot! That Jungle fever goes away, honey, and then what are you gonna do? I say that now in hindsight, because Dennis was afraid to marry me at first. We were acting as husband and wife and having so much fun I didn't care that we weren't married. Our little room on 129th off Seventh was smack dab in the middle of all the action in Harlem. There were parades and dignitaries marching all up and down Seventh Avenue back in those days. Adam Clayton Powell used to stand on a podium right on 125th Street and make political speeches. Malcolm X, too. On Saturdays we'd go to the Apollo Theater, and if you got there by eleven A.M. you could sit there all day through three shows. They'd start with newsreels on the war, comedy shorts, cartoons, or sometimes a movie western with Hoots Tebicon, or a musical with Jeanette MacDonald and Nelson Eddy. Then at one P.M. they played the Apollo theme song, "I Think You're Wonderful," and the bands would bust loose, Count Basie, Duke Ellington, Jimmie Lunceford, Louis Jordan, Billie Holiday, Billy Eckstine. Those musicians worked like slaves, three shows a day. Then on Sunday we'd go to the Metropolitan Baptist Church on 128th and Lenox Avenue to hear Rev. Abner Brown preach.

That man was the finest preacher I've ever heard to this day. He could make a frog stand up straight and get happy with Jesus. You never heard anything like him. He was not fire and brimstone. He brought God into your everyday life in a way that made you think heaven was right next door. Harlem loved him. Metropolitan was the church in Harlem back then. Abyssinian was a big church too, but they'd line up along 128th Street to get into Metropolitan like it was a rock concert. If you didn't get out on that sidewalk by nine A.M. on Sunday morning for the eleven A.M. service, you had to stand in the aisles, and the place seated maybe, I don't know, at least two thousand people. They'd hold two services at the same time, one in the big church upstairs and one downstairs, that's how crowded it was. Dennis was a deacon and he sang in the church choir. And it was a mighty, mighty choir too. What a time it was. Those were my glory years.

My world expanded because of Dennis. He taught me about things I'd never heard of. He meditated every day for fifteen minutes. He did that for years, so that even the children learned to accept that ritual. He believed in equal rights, in knowledge, in books; he taught me about people like Paul Robeson, Paul Lawrence Dunbar, and Joe Louis. He loved the Brooklyn Dodgers—Don Newcombe, Roy Campanella, and Jackie Robinson, especially Jackie Robinson. He couldn't stop talking about him. "Jackie Robinson proved the Negro can play," he said. I learned how to eat my main meal in the evening instead of in the afternoon. Instead of eating kosher, using different table settings for every meal and eating all meat or all dairy dishes, I just ate what I wanted. I tasted pork chops and loved them. Grits, eggs, biscuits, and butter, bacon, collard greens, ham hocks, all the food I couldn't eat before, I ate. But see, I couldn't iron or clean house or cook. I had never learned to cook as a girl. I worked in the store all day while Mameh cooked kosher, or Tateh would hire a black lady to come in twice a week to help Mameh cook. My husband cooked better than I did, and when I stayed home after our first baby I had to learn to cook from my black friends Susie Belton and Irene Johnson. Susie Belton and her husband, Edward, had a room right next to ours in Harlem and Susie's room was always spotless, with curtains and lace across the window and bed, whereas my place always looked like thunder hit it.

In 1942, a few months after my mother died, I told Dennis, "I want to accept Jesus Christ into my life and join the church." Dennis said, "Are you sure you want to do this, Ruth? You know what this means?" I told him, "I'm sure." I was totally sure.

A few Sundays later we were at Metropolitan and they were singing "I Must Tell Jesus," and the spirit filled me and when Rev. Abner Brown asked if anyone wanted to join Metropolitan in Christian fellowship I stepped into the aisle and walked to the front of the church. Rev. Brown shook my hand and all the deacons shook my hand and I have never turned back since. I accepted Jesus that day and He has never let me down from that day to this. I later got on as the church secretary, typing out letters for Rev. Brown, and sometimes witnessing weddings which he held in his office, because I'd be the only one around and you needed two witnesses for a wedding. Watching all these weddings made me long for my own. Here I was a church secretary and Dennis was a stout deacon and we weren't even married. That was a scandal I couldn't live with. I told Dennis one night, "We have to get married," but he was hesitant. He said, "I grew up in the South and I can be killed down there for marrying a woman of the other race." I said, "This isn't the South. This is New York, and I'm a new Christian before God and I'm not living in sin anymore." I told him I was leaving if we didn't get married. That tied him up. He hemmed and hawed so long I actually went out and put a deposit on a room, and when I did that he said, "You don't have to do that, Ruth.

I love you and I'd like you to marry me if you would." What a man he was. I loved him. He was the kindest man I've ever known. All his friends from North Carolina who lived in Harlem would come see him. They'd holler up to our window. "Dennis . . . Dennis!" and he'd invite them in and give them our last food or the shirt off his back if they asked. He came from a home where kindness was a way of life. I wanted to be in this kind of family. I was proud to join it, and they were happy to have me.

We had to meet at city hall to get our marriage license on a Saturday because we both worked during the week. Dennis had to work that Saturday morning also. He had quit my Aunt Mary's by then and was working for the McCoy Publishing Company, a mail order business that supplied emblems, aprons, and books to the Masonic Order. We arranged to meet in front of city hall at two o'clock. I was there at two on the dot and I waited about an hour. Just as I started to walk away thinking, "I thought so," he appeared. "You won't get rid of me that easy," he said.

There were a lot of stares and whispering and pointing and silly questions when we went to the marriage bureau to get our license. The clerks were very nasty and no one wanted to write up our paperwork, but we didn't let those fools ruin our marriage. We got the license and Rev. Brown married us in his private office at the church. I had told him the truth about me and Dennis not really being married and he said, "Don't worry. I'll marry you and be quiet about it." It wasn't till later I discovered several church members had lived together for years as husband and wife and had never gotten married. Some even had grown kids. And Rev. Brown had married them all after the fact, so this was nothing new to him. The church janitor and another helper of the church were our witnesses. Afterwards we had our reception over on 103rd and Third at our friends' apartment, Sam and Trafinna "Ruth" Wilson. They decorated the apartment with pink and white tissue streamers and laid out beautiful trays of delicate sandwiches, entrées, cake, and coffee, and Rev. Brown stopped over to join us. It was a lovely reception, just the five of us. I didn't need a million roses and a marching band. My husband loved me and I loved him, that's all I needed. We were sitting in Ruth's house having coffee at our reception and my husband (oh, I was proud to say it too—"my husband") said to me, "We have to be strong. You know what people will say about us, Ruth. They'll try to break us up." I said, "I know. I'll be strong," and over the years we were tested, but we never split up or even spent a night apart except when he took the kids to North Carolina to see his parents. I never could go south with him because of the danger. The first time I went south with him was the last time, when I took his body down there to bury him.

After we had our first baby in 1943, we moved across the street to a one-room kitchenette that cost six dollars a week. We had a sink, bed, dresser, stove, and a little icebox that the guy came around and put ice in once a week. All our furniture was stuff we'd found or we bought from Woolworth and could be folded: folding chairs, folding tables. Our window faced an alley and the brick wall of the next building and it was so close to the adjoining building you couldn't tell whether it was raining or snowing outside. You had to stick your head out the window to see what the weather was. The bathroom was in the hallway and used by all the tenants and there were roaches everywhere. No matter how many you killed, they kept coming back. I kept my church hat on a shelf in a hatbox, and every Sunday when I'd pick it up to take my hat out, roaches would crawl out. We had four kids in that one room. We used the dresser drawers as cribs and the kids slept with us or on fold-out cots. We lived in that one room for nine years, and those nine years were the happiest years of my life.

I met an interesting white woman during that time, my friend Lily. I saw her in the park on 127th one day while I had my kids out and she had her two kids with her. She was white and her children looked like mine, so we started talking. She was Jewish, from Florida. Her family was rich and she was very refined—Lily was into books and opera—and we had black husbands, so we had that in common. Lily's husband was West Indian, and they were members of the Communist Youth Movement. Back then that was like—boom!—trouble, maybe the government was looking out on them or something. Me and Dennis weren't for communism. We were for Jesus Christ. Lily and I were friends for a long time till she moved away to California. Her husband left her for a younger woman—she was too good for him anyway. He chased around anything in a skirt, in fact chased me around when she wasn't looking but I wouldn't have it. She became a Hare Krishna or one of those wild religions and later she got married again, this time to a white man. I was supposed to go visit her back in the seventies, but just before I did she wrote me a nasty letter saying don't come, and a lot of other mean, insulting things, so I called my trip off and never heard from her again. I don't know why she did that. I think she might have had some problems with her children. That might have been at the bottom of it, because over the years we wrote and I always talked about mine. But her kids had some problems.

Our family grew so fast, before I knew it me and Dennis and four kids were cramped in that one room. So we applied to get an apartment in the Red Hook Housing Projects in Brooklyn. They put us on a long waiting list and said, "Don't expect much," because to get in there was a political thing, but God made a way for us and we got in there in 1950. They gave us a two-bedroom apartment on the sixth floor of 795 Hicks Street with a bathroom. That was the greatest part about it. To have your own bathroom. The floors and walls were pure cement. The kids would get scuffs and big bruises from falling on it, and the glasses and plates had to be replaced with plastic ones because once you dropped them they smashed. But Red Hook was beautiful in those days. It was integrated—Italians, Puerto Ricans, Jews, and blacks. There was grass on the center mall, and a playground with slides and monkey bars. It was a real American life, the life I'd always dreamed of. I'd kiss Dennis in the mornings when he left for work, and when he came home in the evening I'd stand by the window and watch him turn the corner and walk down the center mall. I remember him clearly—his walk, his white shirt, his shoes. The kids would run down to meet him and wrap around his legs like puppies. He would bring groceries from the A&P and a surprise for the kids—a cupcake from his lunch or chewing gum. I loved that man. I never missed home or my family after I got married. My soul was full.

We went to Metropolitan for a couple of years after moving to Red Hook, but Rev. Brown had died of a sudden heart attack and it became too much to ride the subway all the way up to Harlem every Sunday with all the kids. Plus Dennis had gotten the calling to preach and said he wanted to start a church. He quit drinking beer and enrolled at the Shelton Bible College and got his divinity degree from there in

1953. Then we went out and invited our neighbors from Red Hook to come to prayer meeting at our house on Wednesday nights and Sunday mornings. Mrs. Ingram, and your godparents the McNairs, the Floods, the Taylors, they were the first ones to come. I'd clear off the table and put a white tablecloth on it and that would be Dennis's pulpit. After that got going good he said he needed to find a church. I said, "How can we afford a church?" With his little salary, we could barely afford to feed our kids—we had gone from four kids to five to six to seven. I mean, after a while they just dropped like eggs and we loved having them, but I couldn't see how we could afford a church with all these kids. Your sister Helen, I didn't have one prenatal visit to a clinic or anything when I had her. I just walked into the hospital and dropped her like an egg and went home. How we fed them, well, it was meal to meal. I shopped at Goodwill for their clothes and for their Christmas gifts, and I'd walk them around and let them play outside. I'd keep two in a stroller and two next to me, and the rest, I just kept them close. God just provided somehow.

Dennis kept poking around till he found an empty building that was cheap near Red Hook. The white man who owned it didn't want to rent it to blacks so I went over there and signed the lease by myself and when the man saw me and your father and your godfather walking in there the next day carrying paint cans and tools to fix it up with he wanted his building back, but it was too late. We named it New Brown Memorial, after Rev. Brown. The new members kept it going strong, and after we got about sixty people together regularly we moved to a building at 195 Richards Street that had heat, because Dennis was constantly toting heaters around in that other building, which was freezing. Our church survived real well until early 1957, when Dennis came home from work with a bad cold. He was so hoarse I made him lie down and rest. He was hoarse in bed about three weeks.

He smoked cigarettes, filterless Lucky Strikes, and he got hoarse from time to time from preaching and the church not having good heat, and plus it was January and cold outside, so I thought nothing of it. But he got so he couldn't get up out of bed and wouldn't eat and ran a fever, so I took him to St. Peter's Hospital. There were a lot of stares in the hospital when we went in there, stares and questions from the doctors and nurses and such, asking, "Who's that?" and, "Are you his wife?" and all this, but I ignored them. I just wanted Dennis to get out and come home because the kids and I missed him. Our entire world revolved around him. The kids would sit and meditate just like him, then brag to each other how they would show him their meditation when he got home. Your sister Rosetta wouldn't let anyone sit in his chair while he was in the hospital, not even me. No one was allowed to.

He seemed to get seriously ill very quickly. One day he was walking around, the next he was hoarse and laid up in the hospital. The doctors didn't know what was wrong with him. Something in his lungs, this one said. Something in his pancreas, the other one said. They put me off when I'd ask. They'd talk about him in a general way to me, then they'd go in the hallway and point at me with their chins and make remarks about me and Dennis which they thought I couldn't hear. I could hear them but I ignored them. I was focused on my husband. Every day when I'd walk home from the hospital, my friend Lillian would stick her head out her window in the projects and ask, "How's Reverend McBride?" I'd say, "He didn't eat today." She'd say, "Well, he's got to get worse before he gets better." Then one day when I passed by her window I was smiling and happy to tell Lillian, "He ate a grapefruit today," and she said, "See, I told you. He's got to get worse before he gets better." But he didn't get better. He got worse and worse, and during this time I missed my period. I had seven kids, and I had no time to think about my period. I thought it was stress because Dennis was in the hospital longer than I wanted him to be, but when I told him about it, he said, "If it's a boy, we'll call him James after my Uncle Jim." And that's how you got named. See, I didn't think he was going to die. I had no idea, but he knew, because he named you, and he'd make remarks like, "I know the Lord Jesus Christ will take care y'all should anything happen to me. Don't worry, Ruth. Just trust in God." I wouldn't hear of such talk and would make him stop it.

Sometimes in the hospital I would go into the hallway and cry so Dennis wouldn't see me, and one night I was standing out there crying and these two white doctors came by and said, "Who are you?" because it was past normal visiting hours. I pointed to Dennis's room and said, "My husband is in there," and they just got so cold and disgusted. They talked about me right in front of my face and walked away.

One afternoon after Dennis had been in there a few weeks, I went to see him and he was getting thin now from not eating, and he said, "Why don't you bring the kids by to see me?" I said, "We shouldn't do that," because they had school, plus they didn't let kids come inside the hospital and I couldn't drag seven kids up there. I really didn't want them to see him ill like that—the oldest of them was thirteen—but they really wanted to see him too, so I said, "Okay. I'll bring them by the window and you can come see them from the window." He was on the second floor. So I went home and got all the kids and brought them down to the hospital and they stood on the street and yelled up for him, "Daddy! Daddy!" and Dennis came to the window in his bathrobe and looked down at them and waved to them, and from the expression on his face, him standing there waving at the children, who were so excited to see him, I got a horrible feeling in my heart. I told myself, "Lord, he won't die, will he? He's my husband. He's my dream. He won't die now, will he, Lord?" I had no idea what to do. It just seemed like it wasn't going to happen. I went home and prayed to the Lord not to take my husband.

And then a few days later he died.

Lord . . . he just died.

I was home and I got a call from a doctor at the hospital about six in the morning. He asked if I was Mrs. McBride. I said I was. He said, "Mr. McBride just passed away." I said, "That's impossible. He wasn't that sick." The doctor said, "He had cancer," and hung up. That's the first time they told me he had cancer. That's the first I ever heard of it. I stood there and looked out the window over the projects. It was April 5, 1957, I remember it to the day. It was just getting to be the break of day. I looked out there, and there was a blackness that came over me. A sinking feeling like I was going right down into blackness. The children woke up and they were huddled together crying and I started to cry. Part of me died when Dennis died. I loved that man more than life itself and at times I wished the good Lord would have taken *me instead of him, because he was a much better person for living than me. He just had so much more to give the world than me. He brought me new life. He revived me after I left my family, brought me to Jesus, opened my eyes to a new world, then passed on himself. Lord, it was hard. Very hard to let him go. I was angry at him for dying for a while afterwards, angry that he left me with all those kids, but more than that, I missed him.*

We buried him down in High Point, North Carolina. I was in shock a lot of the time, really, and it was your Aunt Candis and your sister Jack who got me and the kids together for the funeral in Brooklyn and then to North Carolina for the funeral down there. It was the first and last time I ever went south with him. I couldn't leave his side after the funeral in Brooklyn and would have ridden with his body in the back of the train if they let me, but they didn't, but I sat on that train and said to myself, "I'm gonna take him home. I will take him home to see him buried," and no white man nor black man would have stopped me from doing it and I swear before God Almighty, had anyone stood before me to prevent me from doing it I would have struck them down. When we got to the train station in High Point, Dennis's Uncle Jim went to claim the body at the counter and I went with him, and the white man at the counter said, "Who's this body for?" I said, "It's for me," and he kept looking at me and Uncle Jim, and he asked us again, "Who's this body for?" and Uncle Jim tried to say the body was with him, so as not to make trouble with that white man, but I told Uncle Jim, "No, Uncle Jim. That is my husband there." I told that man, "That is my husband and I've come here to bury him and he is with me." It caused a little commotion but he gave us no trouble and signed it over to me and Uncle Jim and we buried Dennis in the Burns Hill Cemetery. I was thirty-six then and had been with Dennis nearly sixteen years and I'd never functioned without him. I remember walking through the projects with my seven kids, crying—I'd just break out in tears in the middle of the day sometimes—and your sister Helen, she was about nine years old then, she said, "Don't cry, Ma. Daddy's up in heaven," and it just made me cry more. It was a hard, hard time.

When we came back to New York after burying Dennis, I opened up our mail-

box and found it full of checks and money orders and cash in envelopes from people in the projects who knew us, and people from Metropolitan Church in Harlem. Dozens of letters with checks and money in them. I'll never forget that as long as I live. Folks sent us oranges and apples and chickens and turkeys and clothes and if someone had anything extra, they just gave it to us. The people at his job, McCoy Publishing, the white people, they sent us money. Your sister Jack and Aunt Candis, who came up from North Carolina to stay with us, and your godparents the McNairs, and the Ingrams, and my old friend Irene Johnson, they all pitched in, but even with their help we struggled.

I was so desperate I went back to my Jewish family to ask for help. I looked up my Aunt Betts who had gotten married to a rich man and was living in a fancy building on the East Side in Manhattan with a doorman. I had to talk my way past the doorman to get inside. When I knocked on the door of her apartment, Aunt Betts opened the door, saw who I was, and slammed the door in my face. I left there and cried openly on the sidewalk. Then I called my sister Gladys, who was living in Queens. "You promised you wouldn't leave," she said. I told her I was sorry. But she wasn't really pleased to hear from me. "Call me tomorrow," she said, but when I called the next day her husband picked up the phone and said, "She doesn't want to speak to you. Don't ever call here again," and he hung up on me. See, they were done with me. When Jews say kaddish, they're not responsible for you anymore. You're dead to them. Saying kaddish and sitting shiva, that absolves them of any responsibility for you. I was on my own then, but I wasn't alone, because like Dennis said, God the Father watched over me, and sent me your stepfather, who took over and he saved us and did many, many things for us. He wasn't a minister like Dennis. He was different, a workingman who had never been late for work in the thirty years that he worked for the New York City Housing Authority, and he was a good, good man. I met him after you were born and after a while he asked me to marry him, and Aunt Candis said, "Marry that man, Ruth. Marry him!" and she'd clean the house spotless and cook up these splendid meals when your stepfather came by, to make me look good. He thought I was making up those tasty yams and pork chops and I can't cook to save my life.

When I told him the truth, he said it didn't matter, that he wanted to marry me any-way, even though his brothers thought he was crazy. I had eight children! But I wasn't ready to marry. I turned him down three times. I took you down to North Carolina to show you to Dennis's parents, Etta and Nash, in late '57—they only lasted four or five years after their only child died—and when I told Grandma Etta I was thinking of marrying again, she said, "God bless you, Ruth, because you're our daughter now. Marry that man." That's how black folks thought back then. That's why I never veered from the black side. I would have never even thought of marrying a white man. When I told your stepfather about how my sister and Aunt Betts treated me, he spoke about them without bitterness or hate. "You don't need them to help you," he said. "I'll help you for the rest of my life if you'll marry me," which I did, and God bless him, he was as good as his word.

24.

New Brown

"Come to God! God's in the blessing business!"

It's the October 1994, fortieth-anniversary gala of the New Brown Memorial Baptist Church, and a deacon stands before the audience to muster them up for prayer. Though New Brown is located in Brooklyn, the sixty parishioners are gathered in this tiny banquet room at the Ramada Hotel at La Guardia Airport in Queens because somebody knew one of the hotel cooks and they gave the church a discount. It isn't the Plaza Hotel four-star service, but it will do. The room is dank, dark, and cold. The meat is lousy, the waiters busy. Somebody came up with the idea of hiring a gospel band with a keyboard player, who wears shades and plays too loud, but no one's complaining. This is a celebratory night and the parishioners are dressed in their best. For forty years New Brown, located in the Red Hook Housing Projects, one of the largest and most neglected housing projects in New York City, has stood strong. For forty years the parishioners have struggled. For forty years they have persevered and spread God's word. This is Mommy's home church. This is the church where I got married. This is the church my father Andrew McBride built.

He never lived to see his dreams fulfilled, but when I thumb through his old brown briefcase filled with his paperwork from forty-five years ago, the notes and papers he left behind reveal a man in constant thought: references to Dostoyevsky, Faulkner, Paul Lawrence Dunbar, Jackie Robinson, and notebooks upon notebooks filled with sermons and Bible verses. His writing was filled with allusions to Chronicles, Isaiah, the Book of John, and Philippians. *Sometimes without conscious realization, our thoughts, our faith, our interests are entered into the past*, he wrote. *We talk about other times, other places, other persons, and lose our living hold on the present. Sometimes we think if we could just go back in time we would be happy. But anyone who attempts to reenter the past is sure to be disappointed. Anyone who has ever revisited the place of his birth after years of absence is shocked by the differences between the way the place actually is, and the way he has remembered it. He may walk along old familiar streets and roads, but he is a stranger in a strange land. He has thought of this place as home, but he finds he is no longer here even in spirit. He has gone on to a new and different life, and in thinking longingly of the past, he has been giving thought and interest to something that no longer really exists. This being true of the physical self, how much more true it is of the spiritual self. . . .* He wrote Bible verses on anything he could find—small slips of paper, the back of train schedules, pay stubs. Next to some of the verses he'd scribbled the names and phone numbers of doctors who he thought might be able to help him, cure him of the lung cancer that got him at age forty-five, but they couldn't help him then. It was his time to go and he knew it.

He left behind no insurance policy, no dowry, no land, no money for his pregnant wife and young children, but he helped establish the groundwork for Ma's raising twelve children which lasted thirty years—kids not allowed out after five o'clock; stay in school, don't ever follow the crowd, and follow Jesus—and as luck, or Jesus, would have it, my stepfather helped Mommy enforce those same rules when he married her. The old-timers at New Brown used to say God honored Rev. McBride. The man died without a penny, yet his children grew up to graduate from college, to become doctors, professors, teachers, and professionals all. It was the work, they said, of none other than Jesus Christ Himself.

At the moment, the lady who helped Jesus Christ shepherd Rev. McBride's children to adulthood—and the surviving founder of the New Brown Memorial Baptist Church—is sitting at the end of a long table on the dais, the only white person in the room, wearing a blue print dress and holding my two-year-old daughter, Azure, in her lap. It took a lot to get Mommy here. She didn't want to come. The church got a fine new minister in 1989, and one of his first acts was to order my father's picture to be taken down from behind the pulpit of New Brown, to be placed in a new vestibule constructed with money from the we-still-need-more church fund, all of which fell into the nebulous category of we're-building-up-God's-house, which meant it might not happen while Mommy is still alive. To compound this, he made the mistake of not formally recognizing her during service when she came to visit the church. That was a huge error on his part that could have been easily remedied: if somewhere between reading the "prayer for the sick and shut in" list and the "happy birthday to our members" list he could have squeezed in a "We welcome our original founder, Mrs. McBride, to church today, can I get an amen," the whole thing would have blown over. But he didn't. Instead he treated her like an outsider, a foreigner, a *white person*, greeting her after the service with the obsequious smile and false sincerity that blacks reserve for white folks when they don't know them that well or don't trust them, or both. I saw that same grin on a black waiter's face when the *Washington Post* once sent me to the White House to cover a Nancy Reagan shindig. A smile for Miss Ann the White Lady. Not good.

Ma was so hurt she resolved never to go back there again, a promise she broke again and again, braving the two-hour subway and train commute from her home in Ewing, New Jersey, to sit in church, the only white person in the room, a stranger in the very church that she started in her living room. In all fairness, the minister *was* new. He hadn't much experience and did not know her. In fact, none of the new people at the church knew her and at some point the man corrected his error, but that, Ma said, was not the point. "These new ministers have no vision," she fumed. "They just want a chicken sandwich. Now your father, he had vision." She compared them all to my father, but there really was no comparison. Those were different times, different circumstances, different men.

For years, Mommy rarely talked about my father. It was as if his death was so long ago that she couldn't remember; but deep inside she saw her marriage to him as the beginning of her life, and thus his death as part of its end, and to reach any further beyond that into her past was to go into hell, an area that she didn't want to touch. In order to steer clear of the most verboten area, the Jewish side, she steered clear of him as well. Her memory was like a minefield, each recollection a potential booby trap, a Bouncing Betty—the old land mines the Viet Cong used in the Vietnam War that never went off when you stepped on them but blew you to hell the moment you pulled your

foot away. But when she did speak of him it always began with reverence and ended with sadness, with her saying, "I never knew how sick
he was." I used to stare at his pictures and wonder what his voice
sounded like until I met my cousin Linwood Bob Hinson from North
Carolina, who looks just like him. "If you want to know what your father was like," Ma said, "talk to Bob." Bob is about forty. He talks
with a pleasant, down-home North Carolina twang. He manages a
post office in a small, all-white town, solving problems for angry
postal customers. Bob was one of sixteen blacks who first integrated
his high school in Mount Gilead, North Carolina, where my father
was born. He is a quiet, humorous, religious man of solid accom-
plishment. He lost his fourteen-year-old son, Tory, in a tragic car accident that sent an entire North Carolina community of blacks and
whites reeling in sorrow, and he comforted others even as his own
heart was torn in two. If my son grows up to be like Bob, I'll be a
happy man.

But everyone can't be like Bob, or Rev. McBride, or even Ruth
McBride. People are different. Times change. Ministers change.
Mommy knows this and despite her personal differences with the new
minister, she didn't want to see what amounted to my father's and her
life's work disappear. So she gathered a few donations from my siblings and came to the dinner, sitting at the end of the dais. Next to
her is the keynote speaker, Hunson Greene, head of the New York
Baptists Ministers Conference and a tremendous speaker, who also
happens to be the brother of Mommy's late best friend Irene Johnson.
When it comes to Jesus, Mommy, who scorns the black bourgeoisie,
has friends in high places.

After a while the young minister mounts the dais and works the
crowd like a warm-up comedian. His remarks are short and funny.
The steak's not bad, he jokes, the vegetables not too rubbery, it's a Sat-

urday night, eat up, y'all, we got church in the morning. He moves down the program swiftly. Three of the scheduled anointed speakers did not show, among them church founders Rev. Thomas McNair, my godfather, and Sister Virginia Ingram, both having pleaded illness or scheduling conflicts. Finally Mommy is called to the podium. The new minister introduces her as "the original founder of our church." He scores big points there. Mommy sets my daughter down, rises, and makes her way to the stage.

It takes her forever to get there.

She's seventy-four now. Her knees don't work that well. The quick bowlegged stride is more of a waddle. The lean, pretty woman I knew as a boy has become a small, slightly stooped, cute, feisty old lady. Her face is still the same, the dark eyes full of pep and fire; the hair is still black, thanks to Clairol hair dye; and because she never drank or smoked, and practices yoga three times a week, she looks ten years younger than she is. But she has heart disease and high blood pressure now and takes medication for both. After her heart disease was diagnosed, my physician brothers wanted to schedule her for further tests with top heart specialists, but she refused. "They're not going to get me," she mused, the amorphous "they" being hospitals, the system, and anything else that "sticks tubes in you and takes your money at the same time." She moves slower now, and stairs are a challenge. Lately she's been given to talking as if she won't be around much longer, prefacing each plan with, "Well, if I'm still here next year, I'd love to see . . ." Disneyland, a grandchild's graduation, Paris again, a new car. Some of it is smoke, some of it not. All of it sends my heart spiraling to the floor. Like most people, I don't know what I'll do when my mother makes that final walk home. When she reaches the podium I snap out of my reverie. In her hand is a crumpled piece of paper containing a half-typed, half-longhand speech. The paper is trembling in her hands. She slowly places the paper down and pulls the microphone closer to her face so that it feeds back a bit. As she does so, every hat, every tie, every spoon in the audience is completely still.

"Greetings to the honorable Reverend Reid and the pulpit guests," she reads in a high-pitched, breathless voice. "New Brown has—" And she stops right away. Whether it's the emotion of the moment or just plain nervousness, it's hard to tell, but Mommy has never given a speech before. Ever. She clears her throat as a chorus of "Amens" and "Go on, honeys" resound about the room. She starts again: "Greetings to the honorable Reverend Reid and the pulpit guests. New Brown has come this far by faith . . ." And this time she plows forward, reckless, fast, like a motorized car going through snowdrifts, spinning, peeling out, traveling in circles, going nowhere, her words nearly indecipherable as she flies through the stilted speech in that high-pitched, nervous voice. Finally she stops and puts a hand over her heart and breathes deeply as an embarrassing silence covers the room. I'm about to rush the stage, thinking she's having a heart attack, when she suddenly ditches the speech, the page fluttering to the floor, and speaks directly to the microphone. "My husband wanted to start a church but we had no money, so he said, 'Let's start it right here in our living room.' We cleaned up the house and set up a pulpit with a white tablecloth and invited the McNairs and the Ingrams and the Taylors and the Floods over. That's how we started."

"*Amen!*" comes from the audience. She's lit the fire now.

"We set up chairs and read the Bible and had service. We didn't have an organ player like Sister Lee. We sang without it. Those were the happiest days of my life, and I want you to know . . ." She stops as tears jump into her eyes.

"*Amen!*"

"Yes!!"

"Tell us what you want us to know, honey."

She starts again: "I want you to know . . ."

"Go on! Tell it!"

She takes a deep breath: "I want to you know you are looking at a witness of God's word. It's real," she said. "It's *real!*" "Amen's" roar across the room as she turns and walks away from the pulpit, the pep back in her stride now, the waddle gone, seventy-four years of life dropping off her like snowflakes as she stands behind her seat on the podium facing the audience, overcome. *"God bless you all in the name of Christ!"* she shouts, striking at the air with her fist and sitting down, her face red, nose red, tears everywhere, in my own eyes as well.

Later on, on the way home in the car, I ask her, "So I guess you're not mad at the new minister now?"

"Leave that man alone," she says, as the streetlights twinkle and wink off her face. "He's doing a good job. They're lucky to have a young minister, the way things are in these churches today. You should be a minister. You ever think about that? But you need foresight. And vision. You got vision?"

I tell her I don't think I do.

"Well, if you don't have it, don't waste God's time."

25.

Finding Ruthie

Back in June 1993, during the course of putting together Mommy's will—something I had to force her to do—the macabre subject of her burial came up. "When I die," she said, "don't bury me in New Jersey. Who wants to be buried in Jersey?" She spoke these words as she was sitting in the kitchen of the home she shares with my sister Kathy in Ewing Township near Trenton, a lovely area of New Jersey.

I said, "We'll bury you in Virginia, next to your second husband."

"Oh no. Don't bury me in Virginia. I ran away from Virginia. I don't want to go back there."

"How about North Carolina? We'll bury you where your first husband is."

"No way. I spent all my life running from the South. Don't put me in the South."

"Okay. New York," I said. "You lived there forty years. You still love New York."

"Too crowded," she sniffed. "They bury them three deep in New York. I don't want to be smushed up under somebody when I'm buried."

"Where should we bury you then?"

She threw up her hands. "Who cares? This is nonsense. I've got nothing to leave y'all anyway except some bills." She got up from the kitchen table, bristling, and snapped, "Bury me *here*, bury me *there*, what are you trying to do, kill me? I don't want no tubes in me whatever you do. A doctor will kill you faster than anything." She reached for the sun visor. "Your sister did this to me," she said.

"Did what?"

"I had a little bump on my face and she made me see this fancy doctor. Now I gotta wear this dumb hat all the time. It makes me look like a rooster."

Doctors found squamous cell cancer in a small mole they removed from Ma's face, a condition caused by too much exposure to the sun. Ironically, it's a condition that affects mostly white people. To the very end, Mommy is a flying compilation of competing interests and conflicts, a black woman in white skin, with black children and a white woman's physical problem. Fortunately the doctors got the mole off in time, but the question of her own mortality is one she seems to be preoccupied with of late, probably because she knows death is the one condition in life she can't outrun. "Death is strange, isn't it?" she wonders. "It's so final. You know time is not promised," she says, wagging a finger. "That's why you better get to know Jesus."

If it takes as long to know Jesus as it took to know you, I think, *I'm in trouble.*

It took many years to find out who she was, partly because I never knew who I was. It wasn't so much a question of searching for myself as it was my own decision not to look. As a boy I was confused about issues of race but did not consider myself deprived or unhappy. As a young man I had no time or money or inclination to look beyond my own poverty to discover what identity was. Once I got out of high school and found that I wasn't in jail, I thought I was in the clear. Oberlin College was gravy—all you could eat and no one telling you what to do and your own job to boot if you wanted one. Yet I laughed bitterly at the white kids in ragged jeans who frolicked on the campus lawn tossing Frisbees and went about campus caroling in German at Christmas. They seemed free in ways I could not be. Most of my friends and the women I dated were black, yet as time passed I developed relationships with white students as well, two of whom—Leander Bien and Laurie Weisman—are close friends of mine today. During the rare, inopportune social moments when I found myself squeezed between black and white, I fled to the black side, just as my mother had done, and did not emerge unless driven out by smoke and fire. Being mixed is like that tingling feeling you have in your nose just before you sneeze—you're waiting for it to happen but it never does. Given my black face and upbringing it was easy for me to flee into the anonymity of blackness, yet I felt frustrated to live in a world that considers the color of your face an immediate political statement whether you like it or not. It took years before I began to accept the fact that the nebulous "white man's world" wasn't as free as it looked; that class, luck, religion all factored in as well; that many white individuals' problems surpassed my own, often by a lot; that all Jews are not like my grandfather and that part of me is Jewish too. Yet the color boundary in my mind was and still is the greatest hurdle. In order to clear it, my solution was to stay away from it and fly solo.

I ran for as long as I could. After I graduated from Oberlin College in 1979 and received my master's degree in journalism from Columbia University in 1980, I began a process of vacillating between music and writing that would take eight years to complete before I realized I could work successfully as a writer *and* musician. I quit every journalism job I ever had. I worked at the *Wilmington News Journal* and quit. The *Boston Globe.* Quit. *People* magazine, *Us* magazine, the *Washington Post.* Quit them all. This was before the age of thirty. I must've had some modicum of talent, because I kept getting hired, but I wore my shirt and tie like an imposter. I wandered around the cities by day, stumbling into the newsroom at night, exhausted, to write my stories. I loved an empty city room, just the blinking terminals and a few deadbeats like myself. It was the only time I could write, away from white reporters, black reporters, away from the synergy of black and white that was already simmering inside my soul, ready to burst out at the most inopportune moments. Being caught between black and white as a working adult was far more unpleasant than when I was a college student. I watched as the worlds of blacks and whites smashed together in newsrooms and threw off chunks of human carnage that landed at my feet. I'd hear black reporters speaking angrily about a sympathetic white editor and I'd disagree in silence. White men ruled the kingdom, sometimes ruthlessly, finding clever ways to gut the careers of fine black reporters who came into the business full of piss and vinegar, yet other white men were mere pawns like myself. Most of my immediate editors were white women, whom I found in general to be the most compassionate, humane, and often brightest in the newsroom, yet they rarely rose to the top—even when compared to their more conservative black male counterparts, some of whom marched around the newsrooms as if they were the second coming of Martin Luther King, wielding their race like baseball bats. They were no closer to the black man in the ghetto than were their white counterparts. They spoke of their days of "growing up in Mississippi" or wherever it was, as proof of their knowledge of poverty and blackness, but in fact the closest most of them had come to an urban ghetto in twenty years was from behind the wheel of a locked Honda. Their claims of growing up poor were without merit in my mind. They grew up privileged, not deprived, because they had mothers, fathers, grandparents, neighbors, church, family, a system that protected, sheltered, and raised them. They did not grow up like the children of the eighties and nineties, stripped of any semblance of family other than the constant presence of drugs and violence. Their "I was raised with nuthin' and went to Harvard anyway" experience was the criterion that white editors used to hire them. But then again, that was partly how I got through too. The whole business made me want to scream.

I had no true personal life in those years. Few dates, few dinners, no power lunches. My college sweetheart, a mixed-race woman from Hyde Park, Chicago—her mother was black and her father Jewish— was the apple of my eye, but I was afraid of commitment then, afraid to have children because I didn't want them to be like me. I drifted away from her and let time and distance do the rest. Since I had no personal life outside of journalism other than music, I soared as a reporter, but I always parachuted out in the end, telling my white editors after a year or two that I had to leave to "find myself, write a book, play my sax," whatever the excuse was. Most black folks considered "finding myself" a luxury. White people seemed to think of it as a necessity—most white people that is, except for that all-important one.

Each time I quit a job, Mommy would do a war dance, complete with chants and dancing, usually beginning with, "*Now* what are you gonna do!? You had a second chance and you threw it out the window! You need a *job!*" Like most mothers, she wielded tremendous power and my staunch resolve would crumble like a sandcastle before her frontal assaults, which were like tidal waves. I'd stave her off and back out of her house, saying, "Don't worry, Ma. Don't worry," disappearing into the underworld labyrinth of the New York music scene for months, playing sax with this or that band, selling a piece of music here and there. I was always moderately successful, and later in life much more so, winning the Stephen Sondheim Award for musical theater composition, working with Anita Baker, Grover Washington, Jr., Jimmy Scott, Rachelle Ferrell, and many others, but the eighties were hard times for me as a composer, and each time I hit a dry spell I'd scurry back into journalism—until February 1988, when I was working for the *Washington Post* Style section and thinking of quitting to go back to music in New York. The *Post* Style section is the top of the line, the elite, the haute cuisine, the green, green grass of heaven for newspaper feature writers, and quitting there is not something you do lightly, not even for a seasoned quitter like me. As I pondered it, Ma called me out of the blue, smelling trouble. "I know you!" she snapped. "You're getting steady money now. And a lot of it. *Don't quit that job!*"

But I did quit, partly because I got tired of running, and partly because the little ache I had known as a boy was no longer a little ache when I reached thirty. It was a giant, roaring, musical riff, screaming through my soul like a distorted rock guitar with the sound turned all the way up, telling me, *Get on with your life:* Play sax, write books, compose music, do something, express yourself, who the hell are you anyway? There were two worlds bursting inside me trying to get out. I *had* to find out more about who I was, and in order to find out who I was, I had to find out who my mother was.

It was a devastating realization, coming to grips with the fact that all your life you had never really known the person you loved the most. Even as a young boy I was used to Mommy hiding her past, and I grew to accept it, and the details of her past got lost as my own life moved forward, which is probably how she wanted it anyway. I never even seriously broached the subject with her until 1977, when I was in college and had to fill out a form that for some reason or other required Ma's maiden name. I called her long-distance, in Philadelphia, to find out, and she was suddenly evasive. "What do you need that for?" she asked. "How come?" She hemmed and hawed awhile longer before finally coming out with it. "Shilsky," she said.

"Can you spell that, Ma?"

"Who's paying for this call? Am I paying for it? Did you call me collect?"

"No."

"You're in college," she snapped. "You can spell. Figure it out yourself." *Click.*

The subject was not broached again until I met Al Larkin, then *Sunday Magazine* editor at the *Boston Globe* in early 1982. Al talked me into writing a Mother's Day piece, which the *Philadelphia Inquirer* was kind enough to run simultaneously, since Ma was living in Philly at the time. The public response to the piece was so overwhelming I decided to delve further, partly to get out of working for a living and partly to expel some of my own demons regarding my brown skin, curly hair, and divided soul. I asked Mommy if she would be interested in doing a book and she said no. I told her it could make me a million bucks. She said, "Okay. If you're rich, I'm rich. Just don't quit your job." So I took a leave of absence from the *Boston Globe* in 1982 and *then* quit. "That was one of the stupidest things you've ever done," she snorted, when I announced I had quit.

I expected to sit down with her and conduct long, rambling inter-
views, listening intently as the painful, fascinating details of her life
came tumbling out. I envisioned her as the wise sage, sitting in a rocking chair, impassively pouring the moving details of her life into my
waiting tape recorder over six weeks, maybe two months, me prodding
her along, her cooperating, cringing, inching along, mother and son,
hand in hand, fighting forward, emotionally wrought, until—behold!
We'd be done six months later, and the world would be graced with
our mighty tome.

Eight years later, I was still getting this: "Mind your own business.
If you think too hard, your mind dries up like a prune. I don't want a
TV special named after me. Leave me alone. You're a nosy-body! I'm
moving out of Philly. Let's pack up the house."

My mother is the only individual I have ever known who has been
in the process of moving for ten years straight. After living in
Delaware for only a year, she bought a small rowhouse in Germantown, Philadelphia, in 1975, settled in, and promptly began the process of looking for another place to move that literally became a
lifestyle. She seemed to know every realtor in Germantown on a first-
name basis. She would rise in the morning, scoot out the door, and
ride around with a realtor all day, looking at houses which she had
neither the money for nor the desire to buy, telling the poor realtor
after the day was done to "call me in a week." She'd then clear out of
town completely, "moving" to Atlanta for three weeks to stay with my
siblings, or just disappear from sight, never to be seen by the realtor
again. The poor guy would call and call, and one of us would finally
break the news to him that Mommy wasn't interested. Sometimes
Mommy would be standing by the phone whispering to us in one ear
while we were running interference for her with the other. "Tell him
I'm not here!" she'd hiss. "Why does he keep bothering me?"

It was typical Mommy neurotic behavior, and I didn't fully understand it till I learned how far she had truly come. For her, her Jewish side is gone. She opened the door for me but closed it for herself long ago, and for her to crack it open and peek inside was like eating fire. She'd look in and stagger back, blinded, as the facts of her own history poured over her like lava. As she revealed the facts of her life I felt helpless, like I was watching her die and be reborn again (yet there was a cleansing element, too), because after years of hiding, she opened up and began to talk about the past, and as she did so, I was the one who wanted to run for cover. I can't describe what a shock it was to hear words like "Tateh" and *"rov"* and "shiva" and "Bubeh" coming from Mommy's mouth as she sat at the kitchen table in her Ewing home. Imagine, if you will, five thousand years of Jewish history landing in your lap in the space of months. It sent me tumbling through my own abyss of sorts, trying to salvage what I could of my feelings and emotions, which would be scattered to the winds as she talked. It was a fascinating lesson in life history—a truth-is-stranger-than-fiction marvel, to say the least. I felt like a Tinkertoy kid building my own self out of one of those toy building sets; for as she laid her life before me, I reassembled the tableau of her words like a picture puzzle, and as I did, so my own life was rebuilt.

Mommy has changed, changed from the time she adopted Christianity back in the 1940s. What's different is that she can face the past now. After years of saying, "Don't tell my business," she reached a point where she now says, "It doesn't matter. They're all dead now, or in Florida," which in her mind is the same as being dead. "I'll never retire to Florida," she vowed. Riding past a graveyard one day, she looked over and remarked, "That's Florida Forever."

Ma settled in to get her college degree in social work from Temple University at age sixty-five. She enjoyed the intellectual back-and-forth, the study, reading different authors—I'd forgotten how bright she was. The constant learning and yearning for knowledge was what helped her finally move away from the bustle of Philadelphia to settle into the quieter, safer suburb of Ewing with my sister Kathy. For a few years, she used her degree to work as a volunteer in a Philadelphia social service agency that helped pregnant, unwed mothers; then she moved on to run a weekly reading group for literate and illiterate senior citizens at the local Ewing library, which she still does today. But that's not enough to keep her busy. Every day she rises, spirits her two grandchildren off to school, and drives around central New Jersey, haggling with merchants at flea markets, taking yoga classes in sweats and Nikes, tooling along in a 1995 Toyota at twenty-seven miles an hour in a fifty-five-mile-an-hour zone, holding up traffic on Route I listening to Bernard Meltzer on WOR-AM or the Howard Stern show. ("Grandma laughs when Howard Stern talks dirty," my niece Maya whispers.) Sometimes she'll get up in the morning and disappear for days at a time, slipping away to her old stomping grounds, the Red Hook Housing Projects, to go to church and see her old friends there. She loves Red Hook. Despite the fact that my siblings often urge her to stay out of the projects, she won't. "Don't tell me how to live," she says. She's always been slightly out of control, my mother, always had the unnerving habit of taking the ship into the air to do loops and spins, then fleeing the cockpit screaming, *"Someone do something, we're gonna crash!"* then at the last dying second slipping into the pilot's seat and coolly landing the thing herself, only to forget the entire incident instantly. She wouldn't recall it for you if you showed her pictures of herself doing it. She wipes her memory instantly and with purpose; it's a way of preserving herself. That's how she moves. Her survival instincts are incredible, her dances with fire always fun to watch. "Ruthie," my sisters affectionately called her. "Ruthie's *crazy.*"

In August 1993, after more than fifty years, Ruthie, aka Ruth McBride Jordan, aka Rachel Deborah Shilsky, finally faced the ghosts of her pasts. She went home to Suffolk, Virginia, with me; my sister Judy, a New York schoolteacher; and my brother Billy, an Atlanta physician, in tow. We drove through the entire town, down Main Street, past the one building in town that had an elevator back in the thirties, past the spot where her old home had been, past the old synagogue and old high school, which were still there. "Nothing's changed," she breathed as we sat in front of the old synagogue, still white, aged, but slightly noble with its four tall columns. Ma stared at the old temple, but refused to get out of the car; she merely looked out the window. "They sure do take care of it," she murmured, then ordered Billy, who was driving, to pull away. She seemed immobile— attentive, reflective, but unmoved—until we pulled into the Portsmouth driveway of one Frances Moody, now Frances Falcone, whom I found after a long search. It took twelve years and a ton of good luck for me to find the mysterious Frances. It was, after all, fifty years since Mommy had been there, and most of the old-timers had gone. Those that remained did not remember or know anyone named Frances. Finally I came across a woman named Frances Holland who told me about two girls who befriended her when she was a new student in the seventh grade at Thomas Jefferson Junior High: Ruth Shilsky and Frances Moody. "Frances Moody's alive, living in Portsmouth somewhere," she said. A search through the directory turned up nothing, and I was empty-handed until I visited the town library in Suffolk and a librarian handed me a slip of paper with a phone number on it. "This is the woman you're looking for," she said.

"She's Frances Falcone now." I thanked her and asked her how she knew. She shrugged. She didn't seem to be friendly or unfriendly, just matter-of-fact. She picked up the phone, dialed a number, and handed me the phone. Frances Moody, now Frances Falcone, was on the other line. "I've been looking for you for years," I said. She laughed. "Come see me, but I might not be able to see *you*," she said. "I had an operation on my eyes yesterday for cataracts." Right away I drove to Portsmouth and met my mother's childhood friend, a slim, brown-haired, soft-spoken woman of Mommy's age whose eyes, it turned out, were working just fine. It seems fitting that Frances Moody, who crossed the line and made a Jewish friend in the 1940s when Jews were unpopular in Suffolk, had married an Italian, Nick Falcone, a wood artisan. "The last time I saw your mother, she gave me a shower for my wedding," Frances said. "That was in 1941."

"I bet you thought you'd never see her again," I said.

"No," she said. "I knew I'd see her again somehow."

As we neared Frances's house in Portsmouth, Mommy began to get nervous and to talk excessively. "Look at these roads," she said. "Not a bump. Not a notch. They fix them down here in Virginia, but you shouldn't speed on them, because the cops here don't play. They don't play, you hear me! Billy, slow down! Oh, my knees hurt. The air-conditioning really bothers my knees. And these seats are too small." Even after we pulled into the driveway of Frances's house and her friend approached, she was babbling away, complaining now. "Oh, I can't get up now. My legs hurt. Help me get up, what the heck are y'all trying to do anyway! Driving so fast like that! You can't drive like that in Virginia, I tell you. Now my knees hurt, and—Frances! Look at how thin you are. Oh, you're so pretty. Oh, I'm crying now. Oh boy, what are y'all trying to do . . ." And she wept as she hugged her friend.

After the trip, she and Frances picked up where their high school friendship left off and remain close today. But Frances is as far back as Ruthie can go. Her reunion with her old friend is one of the small, beautiful side benefits of a book experience that Mommy was truly never interested in, exploring a past for her that in many ways is gone forever and is better left buried and untouched.

There are probably a hundred reasons why Ruthie should have stayed on the Jewish side, instead of taking New Jersey Transit and the F train to go to a Christian church in Red Hook, Brooklyn, with her *shvartse* children and friends, and I'm sure the Old Testament lists them all, but I'm glad she came over to the African-American side. She married two extraordinary men and raised twelve very creative and talented children, and I ought to list their names now. After all, that was part of the deal on my end, and her children's achievements are her life's work anyway. So, from eldest to youngest:

ANDREW DENNIS MCBRIDE, B.A., Lincoln University; M.D., University of Pennsylvania Medical School; M.A., Public Health, Yale University; Director of Health Department, City of Stamford, Connecticut.

ROSETTA MCBRIDE, B.A., Howard University; M.S.W., Social Work, Hunter College; Staff Psychologist, New York City Board of Education.

WILLIAM MCBRIDE, B.A., Lincoln University; M.D., Yale University School of Medicine; M.B.A., Emory University School of Business; Medical Director Southeast Region, Medical and Scientific Affairs, Merck and Co., Inc.

DAVID MCBRIDE, B.A. Denison University; M.A., History, Columbia University; PhD., History, Columbia University; Chairman of Afro-American History Department, Pennsylvania State University.

HELEN MCBRIDE-RICHTER, R.N., Hospital of the University of Pennsylvania; G.O.N.P., Emory University School of Medicine, Graduate Student in Nurse Midwifery, Emory University School of Nursing.

RICHARD MCBRIDE, U.S. Army veteran, B.A., Cheney University, Chemistry; M.S., Drexel University; Associate Professor of Chemistry, Cheney State; Chemistry Research Associate, AT&T.

DOROTHY MCBRIDE-WESLEY, A.A., Pierce Junior College; B.A., La Salle University; medical practice office manager, Atlanta, Georgia.

JAMES MCBRIDE, B.A., Oberlin College; M.S.J., Journalism, Columbia University; writer, composer, saxophonist.

KATHY JORDAN, B.A., Syracuse University; M.S., Education, Long Island University; special-education teacher, Ewing High School, Ewing, New Jersey.

JUDY JORDAN, B.A., Adelphi University; M.A., Columbia University Teachers College; teacher, JHS 168, Manhattan.

HUNTER JORDAN, B.S., Computer Engineering, Syracuse University; computer consultant, U.S. Trust Corporation, Ann Taylor.

HENRY JORDAN, junior at North Carolina A&T University; customer service and purchasing, Neal Manufacturing, Inc., Greensboro, North Carolina.

RUTH JORDAN, B.A., Temple University, 1986.

Mommy's children are extraordinary people, most of them leaders in their own right. All of them have toted more mental baggage and dealt with more hardship than they care to remember, yet they carry themselves with a giant measure of dignity, humility, and humor. Like any family we have problems, but we have always been close. Through marriage, adoptions, love-ins, live-ins, and shack-ups, the original dozen has expanded into dozens and dozens more—wives, husbands, children, grandchildren, cousins, nieces, nephews—ranging from dark-skinned to light-skinned; from black kinky hair to blond hair and blue eyes. In running from her past, Mommy has created her own nation, a rainbow coalition that descends on her house every Christmas and Thanksgiving and sleeps everywhere—on the floor, on rugs, in shifts; sleeping double, triple to a bed, "two up, three down," just like old times.

Every year we argue over where to have Christmas. Every year we spend hundreds of dollars on phone calls and letters, writing, faxing, cajoling, and bribing, trying to get out of the pilgrimage to Mommy's tiny house in Ewing. Every year, all twelve of us claim we're going to have Christmas at *our own house* and we're *not* going to travel a *zillion* miles with a *zillion* children to sleep with a *zillion* people on the floor of Ma's like we're little kids, because we're just tired, man, and we did this last year. But at age seventy-four, the president, CEO, and commander in chief of this here army still has the power. My wife, Stephanie, tells a funny story about the first time she came home with me for Christmas and met my family. We were sitting around Ma's house in Ewing, all twelve siblings, doctors, professors all—the house as wild as it always was when we were little, our kids going crazy and our spouses numb, while Mommy's original dozen fell back into nutty behavioral patterns that would make a psychologist throw up his hands in despair—when someone shouted over the din, "Let's go to the movies!" Instantly the room sprang into overdrive.

"*Good idea!*"

"*Yeah . . . let's go. I'll drive.*"

From another room: "*Wait for me!*"

"*Hurry up! Where's my shoes?*"

Mommy was sitting on the living room couch while all this was happening, her feet resting on the coffee table. She yawned and said softly, "I want to eat."

The movie was instantly forgotten.

"Yeah! Let's eat!"

"I sure am hungry!"

"Let's order out!"

From another room: *"I been waiting to eat all day . . . !"*

Now that's what you call power.

Epilogue

In November 1942, a twenty-one-year-old Jewish woman named Halina Wind was sent by her parents into hiding after the Nazis marched into her home village of Turka, Poland, and murdered most of the town's six thousand Jews, eventually killing her parents, a brother, and grandmother. Halina Wind fled to the city of Lvov, where she and nine other Jews hid in a sewer for fourteen months, living admidst rats and sewer filth in a wet, underground prison, never seeing the sunlight, fed by three Polish sewer workers. Halina Wind survived that horror and lived to tell the world of it.

In 1980—nearly forty years later—Halina's only son, David Lee Preston, a tall, thin, handsome dude with a lean face, dark eyes, and glasses, wandered over to my desk at the *Wilmington* (Del.) *News Journal* holding a story I had written about boxer Muhammad Ali. He was a reporter at the paper like I was, but we had never met.

"This is an excellent piece," he said.

"Thanks," I said.

"You spelled Muhammad wrong. It's with an 'a' at the end, not an 'e.' The copy desk missed it." The copy desk is supposed to catch those kinds of errors before they make the paper.

"Okay." I shrugged. No sweat off my back.

"I heard you're a sax player," he said. "You ever heard of Albert Ayler?"

Albert Ayler was an amazing, avant-garde saxophonist known only to the most die-hard jazz enthusiasts. Rumor has it he disappeared into Manhattan's East River wearing cement shoes. I was completely surprised. "How'd you hear of him?" I asked.

He shrugged and smiled. From that day to this, Halina Wind's son has been one of my best friends. I didn't know David Preston was a Jew when I first met him. He didn't wear it on his sleeve. He was a compassionate, curious, humorous intellectual, a great writer, and his religious background never came up, nor did it seem important to me at the time. Only when I revealed to him that my mother was the daughter of an Orthodox Jewish rabbi did his Jewish background emerge, because he understood the true depth of Mommy's experience immediately. "What a woman," he said. This from a guy who was raised by an amazing woman himself.

As his life moved forward—today he is writing a book about his mother and working as the South Jersey columnist for the *Philadelphia Inquirer*—so did mine. I asked him to be in my wedding when I married my African-American wife, Stephanie, in 1991. He asked me to do the same when married his Jewish wife, Rondee, the following year.

He also wanted Mommy to come to his wedding. I agreed to ask her for him, though privately I had my doubts.

"Interesting." That was her response when I put it to her.

"He really wants you to come," I said. I knew she liked David immensely.

"I'll come if Kathy comes with me," she said. Ma likes her daughters to come with her for anything emotional. Her sons she likes to brag about and say what great things they've done, and what schools they've gone to, and on and on, but in truth it's the women of the McBride-Jordan clan who hold the family together and will do so after she is gone. Like Mommy, my sisters have learned to absorb punishment and get up off the ground after the shock of life's blows wears off. The men, yours truly included, wallow about as life's details mow us down and lay us out on Mommy's couch to watch Bowl games when the family gathers at Christmas and Thanksgiving, no matter how lousy the games are. Kathy agreed to come to the wedding with her nine-year-old daughter, Maya, and we were on.

It was held at Temple Beth Shalom in Wilmington, where Halina Wind Preston had taught for three decades. I was an usher in the wedding, and as I marched down the aisle wearing a black tuxedo and a white yarmulke, behind six Jewish musicians who played the traditional Israeli folk song "Erev Shel Shoshanim," I felt somber, moved, and proud. David Preston married his wife with the kind of gusto and enthusiasm and seriousness with which he attacks everything in life. They signed a contract. They were married under a *huppah,* a wedding canopy. Two cantors, one of whom was David's sister, Shari Preston, stepped forward and sang. David's uncle, Halina Wind's brother, Rabbi Leon Wind, presided over the ceremony, and spoke eloquently, with reverence and power. "My heart is filled with deep and conflicting emotions today," the seventy-eight-year-old rabbi said. "I'm overjoyed that your marriage has come. Yet my heart aches because my sister, for whom this would have been the supreme moment of her life, did not live to see it." David's mother, Halina Wind Preston, died after open heart surgery in December 1982 at the age of sixty-one. The rabbi's heartfelt words moved the entire congregation, and my thoughts traveled to my own Jewish mother, who was sitting in the fourth row.

I turned to peek as Mommy wiped her reddening nose with a handkerchief, a camera strapped around her wrist. At moments like this she usually likes to shoot pictures. She catches all of her important moments with a camera, waddling down Brooklyn's Atlantic Avenue from the A train to Long Island College Hospital to take pictures of my daughter Azure's first days of life; standing my toddler son, Jordan, up against a tree in her yard so she can snap a quick picture of him in his Easter outfit. Her photos are horrible, heads cut off, pictures of nothing, a table, a hand, a chair. Still, she shoots pictures of any event that's important to her, knowing that each memory is too important to lose, having lost so many before. However, she is snapping no pictures now. She's staring straight ahead, wearing a white dress with a necklace this rainy afternoon, her long nose and dark eyes seeming to blend in perfectly with the mostly eastern European faces surrounding her. She'd had no problems walking into the synagogue. She looked about the lobby and nodded her approval. Oh yes, this is the memorial wall where they put the names of the ones who died, she pointed out. Oh yes, the men will leave the room if a woman cantor performs. She talked as if she were visiting a museum.

"How do you feel being here?" I asked her.

"I feel fine," she said. "I'm happy to see David getting married. He's a nice Jewish boy." She laughed at the irony of it. I realized then that whoever had said kaddish for Mommy—the Jewish prayer of mourning, the declaration of death, the ritual that absolves them of responsibility for the child's fate—had done the right thing, because Mommy was truly gone from their world. In her mind, she was a guest here. "I don't have this left in me anymore," she remarked at one point.

Downstairs at the reception following the ceremony, Mommy perked up even more as the klezmer musicians played traditional Jewish folk songs. She ate kosher hummus, tahini, and baba ghanouj, and explained the importance of kosher food to my niece Maya; she laughed and joked with a group of Jewish ladies who sat next to us, and even got up to watch me help other men place David Preston in a chair, lift him up, and carry him around the room in the traditional Jewish men's wedding dance. But not long after, she came back to our table and announced, "It's time to go," in a tone and manner that said she really was ready to leave.

When we opened the synagogue door, it was raining outside and we had no umbrellas. Kathy and Maya made a quick dash for the car, running ahead while Mommy and I followed. "That's how it's done," Ma said as I helped her down the synagogue stairs, her arthritic knees aching in the damp weather. "That's how the old Jews did it in my day too. You marry under that thing, the *huppah*. You break the glass. You know that could've been me," she said as she took the last stair and her foot landed shakily on the sidewalk.

"I know," I said, releasing her arm and walking toward the car, "and where would that have left me . . . ?" But suddenly I was talking to myself. She was gone. I stopped and turned to look behind me. She was standing in front of the synagogue entrance, staring up at the doorway from the sidewalk, lost in thought, the rain billowing into puddles around her. She stood there for a moment in the downpour staring thoughtfully, before turning and hurrying toward the car, her bowlegged waddle just the same as it always was.

Thanks and Acknowledgments

My mother and I would like to thank the Lord Jesus Christ for His love and faithfulness to all generations. Thanks to my loving wife, Stephanie Payne, who stood me up when I could no longer stand, who would not let me back away from the dream, who made me a man. To my children, Jordan and Azure, that they might know where they came from.

To my eleven brothers and sisters: Dr. Andrew Dennis McBride, Rosetta McBride, Dr. William (Billy) McBride, Dr. David McBride, Helen McBride-Richter, Richard McBride, Dorothy McBride-Wesley, Kathy Jordan, Judy Jordan, Hunter Jordan, and Henry Jordan. Thank you for your help in putting this book together and keeping us strong over the years. To my special sister, Jacqueline Nelson of Louisville, Kentucky, who helped me turn my life around.

Thanks to my editor, Cindy Spiegel, at Riverhead, whose creativity, imagination, guidance, hard work, and foresight created the organization and magic of this book, and to my agent, Flip Brophy, of Sterling Lord Literistic, who stuck with me for ten years despite the fact that I never made her a dime.

My mother and I would also like to thank our friends and family in Harlem, in the Red Hook Housing Projects in Brooklyn, in St. Albans, Queens, and in Philadelphia, who stuck with us over the years: in particular my godparents, Mother Rachel and Rev. Tom McNair and family; Mother Virginia Ingram and family; Rev. Edward Belton and family of Passaic, New Jersey; the late Irene Johnson, her daughters Deborah and Barbara, her sister Vera Leake, her brother Rev. Hunson Greene, and the rest of her family; Rev. Elvery Stannard, Rev. Arnet Clark and Tiberian Baptist Church; Pastor Joseph Roberts and Ebenezer Baptist Church; Dr. Gary Richter, Rose McBride, Rebecca Randolph; Gladys and Fred Cleveland, Alice and Neddie Sands, Dorothy and Thomas Jones. The Napper and Harris families, Sheila Warren and Evelyn Hobson; Trafinna "Ruth" Wilson and family of Wilmington, Delaware; our late beloved Aunt Sallie Candis Baldwin and Etta and Nash McBride; the Hinson, Leake, and Rush families of Mount Gilead, North Carolina; Aunt Mag Lomax, Cousin Edna Rucker and the Gripper family of High Point, North Carolina; the New Brown Memorial Baptist Church in Brooklyn; Rev. Thomas Davis of Crossroads Baptist Church in Harlem; Cousin Maggie Harris and family of Richmond, Virginia; Thelma Carpenter, Uncle Walter Jordan, Flossie Jordan, and the Jordans of Brooklyn and Richmond; and the Payne and Hawkins families in Los Angeles.

Thanks to the folks in Suffolk, Virginia: Frank and Aubrey Sheffer, Helen Weintraub, the late Aubrey Rubenstein, Mrs. Frances Holland, Mary Howell-Read of the city clerk's office, Curly Baker, and Eddie Thompson. A heartfelt embrace to Frances and Nick Falcone of Portsmouth, Virginia, for reentering our lives. Thanks to Dina Abramowicz of the Yivo Institute for Jewish Research in New York City and to all the brothers on the Corner at Vermont Liquors in Louisville, especially Mike Fowler, Big Richard Nelson, and the late Chicken Man. Thanks to tax accountant Milton Sherman, Janette Bolgiani, and Julian "Sharon" Jones. Thanks to Jim Naughton at the *Philadelphia Inquirer*, Rhonda Goldfein, Holocaust survivors Halina Wind and George Preston and their son David Preston, who helped reveal the wonders of Judaism for me. Thanks to my friends at the *Boston Globe:* Dennis Lloyd, Al Larkin, Jack Driscoll, Ed Siegel, Cindy Smith, Steve Morse, and of course Ernie Santosuosso. Thanks to Mary Hadar, who was a guiding editor at the *Washington Post,* and bebop guitarist Jeff Frank, whose second career still awaits. Thanks to Jay Lovinger and Gay Daley, who read my manuscript and whose kindness has always been an inspiration to me and my family. Thanks to Bill Boyle, Mike Daley, Hank Klibanoff, Marguerite Del Giudice, Doran Twer, Gar Joseph, Gary Smith, and Sally Wilson; thanks to Isabel Spencer and Fred Hartman, who gave me my first journalism job, to Norman Isaacs, who taught me to be good enough to get one, to Jann Wenner of *Rolling Stone/Us* magazines, who let me practice my soprano sax at work, no problem, and to Eric "Bud Powell" Levin, Jesse Birnbaum, Pat Ryan, Jim Gaines, and Mercedes Mitchell at *People.* Thanks to Jill Nelson, Richard Ben Kramer, Carolyn White, Gerri Hirshey, and living legend and author John A. Williams, whose life's work is an inspiration to all writers. Thanks to Anita Baker and Walter Bridgeforth, whose generosity helped me survive the lean years, jazz legend Jimmy Scott, who taught me to swing, saxophonist Grover

Washington, Jr., Gary Burton, Everett Harp, my homie Damon Due White, my homegirl Rachelle Ferrell, Gerard Harris, writing partner Ed Shockley, Larry Woody, Sy Friend, and Vinnie Carrissimi, who still can't jump; to George Caldwell, musical partner Pura Fé, Dana Crowe, Lisa Hartfield Davé, Professor Wendell Logan, Fred Nelson III, Laurie "Colgate" Weisman, Roz Abrams, and the Rouet family of France. Finally, thanks to the Bien family of Concord, New Hampshire, and their sons Alec and Leander, who sat up for many nights listening to me recite my dreams, then stood by me in the reality of the hard days that followed.

"In all thy ways acknowledge Him and He shall direct thy paths." Proverbs, 3:6

James McBride

James McBride is a writer, composer, and saxophonist. A former staff writer for the *Wilmington (Del.) News Journal*, the *Boston Globe*, *People*, and the *Washington Post* (Style Section), he has also written for the *Philadelphia Inquirer*, *Rolling Stone*, *US*, and *Essence*. James is the 1993 recipient of the American Music Theater Festival's Stephen Sondheim Award for his work in musical theater composition, including the highly acclaimed jazz/pop musical "Bobos." He has written songs for Anita Baker, Grover Washington, Jr., and Gary Burton, among others, and often tours as a sideman with legendary jazz vocalist Jimmy Scott. A graduate of Oberlin College, he holds a master's degree in journalism from Columbia University. He is married with two children and lives in South Nyack, New York.

Ruth McBride Jordan

Ruth McBride Jordan was born Rachel Deborah Shilsky (Ruchel Dwajra Zylska) in Poland, in 1921. Her family immigrated to America when she was two, and eventually settled in Suffolk, Virginia. After high school she moved to New York City and married Andrew D. McBride, with whom she founded the New Brown Memorial Baptist Church in Brooklyn, New York. After her husband's death in 1957, she remarried, to Hunter Jordan, who died in 1972. She is a 1986 graduate of Temple University in Philadelphia, where she received her degree in Social Work Administration at age 65. Today Ruth travels to Paris, London, New York, and Atlanta regularly; works as a volunteer with the Philadelphia Emergency Center, a shelter for homeless teenage mothers; runs a reading club in the Ewing, New Jersey, public library; and works at the Jerusalem Baptist church in Trenton, New Jersey, in their program to feed the homeless. She lives in Ewing township with her daughter Kathy Jordan and Kathy's two children, Gyasi and Maya. She has twelve children and twenty grandchildren